Capitol Murder

or

Capital Mayhem?

CAPITOL MURDER
OR
CAPITAL MAYHEM?

by

Caroline R. Miller

LITTLE MIAMI PUBLISHING CO.
Milford, Ohio
2014

Little Miami Publishing Co.
P.O. Box 588
Milford, Ohio 45150-0588
www.littlemiamibooks.com

Cover design by BrandingGround LLC

Printed in the United States of America on acid-free paper.

ISBN-13: 978-1-941083-01-7

Library of Congress Control Number: 2013958092

To my grandmother Mary A. Taulbee Rose and all Taulbee family members who reside throughout the nation but continue to call Kentucky home.

"Marble statues and elaborate paintings tend to dominate tours of the U.S. Capitol, but for those so inclined, a stopover can include blood-stained stairs from a century-old gunfight."

—ABCNEWS.com: "Ghosts of the Capitol"

Contents

Acknowledgments

No book or compilation of historical facts and narratives can be successfully completed without the aid of several persons and institutions and their archives. Fortunately, in this decade researchers have almost instant access to data and pictures using the Internet. However, there are times when the search for information takes writers to books, microfilm, and even microfiche which remain in some libraries. Two collections of regional documents and reels can be located at the Ripley Union Library in Ripley, Ohio, and Morehead State University in Morehead, Kentucky. Both are fortunate to have outstanding librarians and archivists—namely, Alison Gibson in Ripley and Rob Sammons at Morehead.

Without the aid of the Bracken County Historical Society archivist and technical advisor, Bill Baker, few pictures accompanying the manuscript would have obtained the best level of clarity. Those images which were not able to be scanned properly were sketched by my sisters, Mary M. Watson of Russellville, Ohio, and Elizabeth A. Taheri of Dallas, Texas. Appreciation always goes to the members and officers of the Bracken County Historical Society in Bracken County, Kentucky, who have graciously allowed me to write and compile historical incidents as well as supported the challenge of publishing a manuscript.

One of my proofreaders, Rita Thomas-Edie, was left stunned at the conclusion of the trial and its incredulous verdict. A former prosecutor, Edward Rudd, also read the manuscript to make certain my interpretations of the procedures used in the lengthy murder trial were accurate. To those who commented on this manuscript, saying thank you seems inadequate to express my sincere appreciation.

Preface

JUST BEFORE HALLOWEEN several years ago, I was watching Dan Rather report the national news and, while taking a lull from covering world crises situations, he delivered his personal version of "the ghost that haunts the Capitol" in Washington, D.C. I listened lightheartedly to his outrageous tale about a ghost that supposedly cavorts nonsensically along the halls of the Capitol along with a demon cat. The highly regarded newsman centered this preposterous scenario on the murder of a former representative from Kentucky named Taulbee.

Because my paternal grandmother was a member of a large eastern and central Kentucky family by that surname, I wanted some answers. All my older family members had passed away, and none of my siblings or cousins knew of the representative, much less the ghost. Coincidentally, I had been teaching high school English for nearly three decades at that time and every year included in my text was the poem "Old Christmas Morning," which told about the shooting of three people, one of whom was named Taulbe. With this spelling variation, I had totally ignored the connection until I began researching both the alleged ghost reference to the Capitol and the allusion to a spirit who was one of the characters in the poem.

Newspapers had not been digitized in the 1980s, but Morehead State University in Kentucky still had drawers of microfiche and a reader in their library. In this collection were several Kentucky newspapers from the 1890s which included articles about the shooting of William P. Taulbee by *Louisville Times* correspondent Charles E. Kincaid. Further research, using census records at Thomas D. Clark History Center in Frankfort, Kentucky, provided me with the information that Representative Taulbee and my great-grandfather were brothers. No one in my generation, with whom I spoke, knew of the tragic murder of this great-great uncle or the century-old apparition ascending and descending the domes and stairways of the Capitol.

Although I must admit I am certainly skeptical about orbs and phantasms sighted by numerous visitors in the Capitol, I find it reasonable to think Taulbee's spirit was not willing to leave without proper adjudication of his assailant. Anyone's death by murder is shocking; therefore, Taulbee's tragic end will continue to be told in songs and other forms of media-rich intrusion into a politician's life.

Authors have included chapters and portions of their books on this ghost or apparition in our nation's Capitol, along with dozens of other sightings. However, my material on this topic and my personal family interest spurred me to tell as completely as possible the entire episode and its concluding trial. Please, not only read with some humor, but also realize the seriousness of this murderous situation in the Capitol—five sons were left without a father, a widow had to suffer the comments and looks of those who believed all sensational news reports, and the life of a once-promising politician from Kentucky was taken in a tragic set of circumstances.

CHAPTER 1

Ghosts Roam the Capitol

RED-JACKETED OFFICIAL TOUR GUIDES are not likely to willingly reveal the government's gory secrets. Nonetheless, one of the more shocking stories they might recall concerns the murder of former Kentucky representative William Preston Taulbee. When shot, the congressman was descending the steps of the House Press Gallery located on the east stairway to the House Chamber of the Capitol. However, some members of the Capitol staff have related their versions of the building's bloodstained steps on the Internet site, "Ghosts of the Capitol," which tantalizes a reader with bits of information about one of the most famous ghosts of our nation. The spirit of William Preston Taulbee is said to remain in the Capitol to continue a feud with the press that did not end when a reporter shot him on February 28, 1890.[1]

Dr. David R. Oester, sponsor of the International Ghost Hunt-

---

1.John Solomon, "A Murder in the Capitol," *The Hill* (Washington, D.C.), 13 October 1999, 1; see also, ABCNEWS.com, "Ghosts of the Capitol," 1, (www.abc-news.go.com/sections/travel/DailyNews/capitol000208.html).NEWS.com.

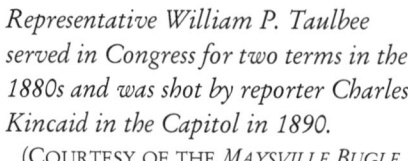

Representative William P. Taulbee served in Congress for two terms in the 1880s and was shot by reporter Charles Kincaid in the Capitol in 1890.
(COURTESY OF THE *MAYSVILLE BUGLE* ARCHIVES.)

ers Society, has remarked, "A lot of the reason the spirits are there is because of emotional attachments of the political process, loving it so much that they never left. Ghost hunters declare the Capitol building is home to no less than fifteen spirits and a demon black cat."[2] This cat is seen by some believers traveling the halls of Congress, making a scene around the time of a domestic disaster or near a presidential inauguration. Steve Livengood, Capitol Historical Society chief tour guide, has also admitted he has seen ghosts in the Capitol.

Two construction workers were perhaps the first to die in the building; one worker's image has been sighted floating under the rotunda dome, carrying a tray of tools. Lawana Holland-Moore, a Washington, D.C., area resident and graduate of George Washington University is a well-known writer and ghost hunter in Washington, D.C. She acknowledged there are several theories concerning why spirits are attracted to certain locations.

> Usually these are places where something tragic or unexpected has happened, places of high emotional energy. It is also believed the energy being left behind is like an imprint, the

2. ABCNEWS.com, "Ghosts of the Capitol," 1; see also James C. Klotter, *Kentucky Justice, Southern Honor, and American Manhood, Understanding the Life and Death of Richard Reid* (Baton Rouge, La.: Louisiana State University Press, 2003), 126.

energy is still present. Some ghosts are very much aware of what's happening, but others believe spirits are caught in a loop and are unaware that times have changed. They're doing what they did before.[3]

Adding to this version is one shared by Michael Judge, a Capitol tour guide, who once remarked, "A friend of mine, a police officer, spent an entire night here one night, and he said unless he was ordered to do so, he would never do it again. He heard some things and saw some things."[4] Judge is reported to be an expert on the Capitol's present and past history and can recite countless details about the grand old building and its construction.

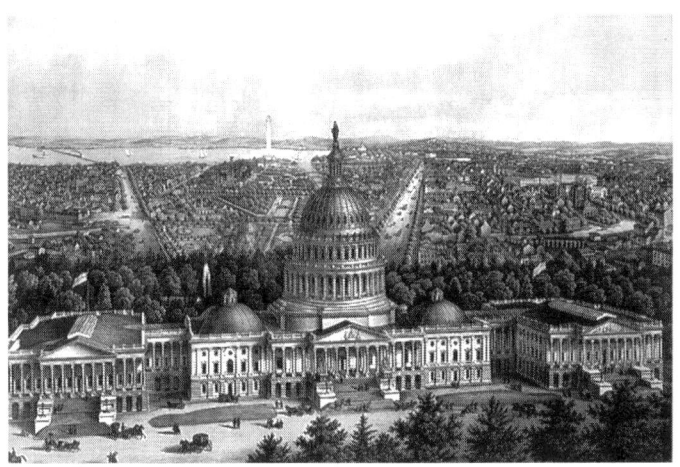

In this view the U.S. Capitol and adjoining District of Columbia give the impression Washington, D.C., was sparsely populated with green spaces between the center of government and the Potomac River.
(COURTESY OF THE LIBRARY OF CONGRESS ARCHIVES.)

As for his knowledge of Representative Taulbee, Judge relates the marble steps leading to the House Press Gallery remain stained

3. ABCNEWS.com, "Ghosts of the Capitol," 1; see also Lisa Dunbar, "Ghost of Kentucky Congressman Reaches out from the Past," *Ledger Independent* (Maysville, Ky.), 25 October 2002.

4. CNNNews, 24 October 2000, 11:30 a.m. EDT (1530GMT) Washington (Reuters), "With Election Looming, Washington is a ghost town—literally." Taken from www.rollcall.com/pages/features/00/wbc/0201/0121h.html.

by the blood of the congressman who was shot by reporter Charles Kincaid. "Every time a reporter trips on those steps, it is said Taulbee's ghost is tripping him as he walks over his blood."[5] According to John Solomon, former Associated Press correspondent to *The Hill* and previous editor-in-chief of the *Washington Times*, the media should certainly watch its step "As elected officials and the media continue to spar over the proper role of private lives in news coverage, journalists covering Congress—particularly on the issue of sex and politics—should beware. The ghost of Congressman Taulbee, legend has it, still appears in the building from time to time to trip passing reporters."[6]

While historical in fact, the Taulbee ghost legend remains a popular topic in modern media. Oester includes a rather accurate image of Taulbee's ghost on his *International Ghost Hunters* website in the "Best of the Best" gallery, as a "picture of a man, somewhat transparent. His face is bold with short-cropped hair."[7] Dan Rather, the noted ABC and CBS news anchor, included his accounting of this ghost each Halloween; although he readily admitted that he had never experienced such a phantasm. The topic of ghosts in our nation's capital city became more widely known after a 2006 A&E documentary, *America's Haunted Houses*, was aired and referenced Taulbee's ghost. Also calling more attention to the Capitol apparitions, Dan Brown's popular 2009 novel, *The Lost Symbol*, set in Washington, D.C., used masonry symbols as its recurring theme. Whether a visitor to the Capitol is a follower of poltergeists or at times spots a glimpse of an unexplainable shadow or orb, most tourists will quickly translate their versions of this tale to others in hopes of some explanation.

John Solomon offered this murder was more than a simple reaction to a newspaper correspondent's unsavory article, "It may

---

5. Ibid.

6. Solomon, "A Murder in the Capitol."

7. David Oester e-mail to Caroline R. Miller, 13 April 2002.

not be unusual for a reporter to write about a politician's extramarital affair. The politician, however, does not normally attempt to take revenge by trying to kill the reporter who wrote the story."[8] In the early weeks of 1890, Taulbee angrily confronted the *Louisville Times*[9] reporter, Charles Kincaid, regarding "nasty things" the journalist had written in 1888 about the politician.[10] Shortly after Taulbee's death, another Kentucky paper, *Winchester Democrat*, followed with more details in an article about the alleged affair. This news account stated the *Louisville Times* was the only newspaper in this or any other state to report Taulbee and the brown-haired Patent Department clerk, Miss Laura Louisa Dodge, were in fact caught in a compromising

SHOT IN THE HEAD.

CHARLES E. KINCAID, OF THE COURIER-JOURNAL.

Shoots Ex-Congressman Pres Taulbee Through the Head for Pulling His Nose.

Associated Press to THE LEADER.

WASHINGTON, Feb. 28.—At 1:45 p. m. ex-Congressman Pres Taulbee, of Kentucky, was shot through the head by Charles E. Kincaid, correspondent of The Louisville Times and The Courier-Journal.

The trouble was caused by the ex-Congressman pulling the correspondent's nose for publishing certain statements in regard to him. The shooting occurred just outside the capitol near the southeastern entrance to the building. Taulbee was shot in the head, but it is not known yet how serious.

"Shot in the Head" was the attention-grabbing headline on Friday, 28 February 1890, which immediately evoked strong reactions to the two-year-old hostility between former representative Taulbee and correspondent Kincaid. (COURTESY OF THE *KENTUCKY LEADER* ARCHIVES.)

position, lunching on forbidden fruit and hidden waters.[11] Miss Dodge had just celebrated her twenty-first birthday on January 9, 1890, barely a month before the shooting. She was the daughter of

---

8. Solomon, "A Murder in the Capitol."

9. "Shot in the Head," *Kentucky Leader* (Lexington, Ky.), 28 February 1890.

10. Ibid.; see also www.ghostweb.com.; see also Tim Krepp, "The Bloody Steps," *Capitol Hill Haunts* (Charleston, S.C.: The History Press, 2012), 28–30.

Asaph and Laura Pentz Dodge and was raised in North Brookfield, Massachusetts, not Kentucky as many major newspapers reported.

According to an exposé published in the *Daily Capital* in Frankfort, Kentucky, during March 1890, the basis for the difficulties between Taulbee and Kincaid began when Representative Taulbee supposedly had Kincaid dropped from the rolls of the doorkeeper, which could have interfered with his abilities as a correspondent. This article continued, "Mr. Kincaid was not the author of the scandalous article as originally published and did not know anything about it till printed in a Washington paper."[12] This disclaimer obviously did not deter the Louisville papers as they continued to include regular columns containing titles such as "Washington Gossip" and "Foreign Gossip." These columns once proposed to their readership, "Washington is in a whirl this winter, socially and politically. The women are swarming here to enjoy the season, and we see many beautiful ones in the round of festivity. There are not enough men to go around by a large majority. Even a piece of a man is in demand."[13]

Laura Dodge and other younger women in the 1890s wore similar dresses and hats while strolling the avenues of Washington, D.C. (COURTESY OF THE KEN-TUCKY LEADER ARCHIVES.)

11. "Hon. Press Taulbee Dies . . . ," *Winchester (Ky.) Democrat*, 19 March 1890, 1; see also "Time Can't Erase Bloodstains . . . ," *Arizona Republic* (Phoenix, Ar.), 25 February 1962, 12-A; see also Robert S. Pohl, *Wicked Capitol Hill: An Unruly History of Behaving Badly* (Charleston, W.Va.: History Press, 2012), 30.

12. "Kincaid-Taulbee," *Daily Capital* (Frankfort, Ky.), 10 March 1890, 2.

13. "Washington Gossip," *Louisville (Ky.) Times*, 16 January 1888, 2; see also "Foreign Gossip," *Louisville (Ky.) Times*, 18 January 1888, 1.

CHAPTER 2

Mountain Orator Shot

Kincaid had been a correspondent in Washington for several years and was author of "lively and gossipy communications," which were widely read at the Capitol.[14] The description of Taulbee's affair was further depicted a century later in a more scintillating manner in Solomon's article, "A Murder in the Capitol." In this interpretation published in *The Hill* were these suggestive references and similes referring to Taulbee's affair: "The thirty-nine-year-old former Methodist minister was developing quite a reputation off the Floor as well. With his wife back in Kentucky, Taulbee was carrying on a torrid relationship with an eighteen-year-old female employee of the U.S. Patent Office, who was described as 'bright as a sunbeam and saucy as a bowl of jelly; petite of figure but plump as a partridge.'"[15] The manner in which modern-day politicians deal with their scandals and affairs differs in each case.

14. "A Distressing Affair," *Daily Capital* (Frankfort, Ky.), 1 March 1890, 1.
15. Solomon, "A Murder in the Capitol."

General Dwight Eisenhower traveled openly with his secretary—many reporters decided it not prudent to discuss their relationship in their columns. President Bill Clinton simply chose to play semantics with his accusers. John Edwards, a former presidential candidate, kept his encounters quiet until a child appeared—casting no doubt to the parentage.

Solomon continued his narrative, which he pulled from the dusty archives of the late nineteenth century newspapers, with these images of the midday trysts: "The little daisy would trip up to him by another stairway. And they would hold sweet communion for half an hour before going to a plebeian Monday lunch."[16] These scandalous words first became public in the early fall of 1888 in the *Washington Evening Star* before being submitted for eager readers in a December 1888 edition of *Washington Post*. The following was the description of the supposed liaison of Taulbee and Dodge:

Ex-Congressman Shot.

Attempted Assassination In the Capitol.

THE VICTIM WAS W. P. TAULBEE

He Pulls the Nose of Charles E. Kincaid, a Newspaper Correspondent, and Receives a Bullet in His Head as a Reward.

WASHINGTON, March 1.—Charles E. Kincaid, correspondent of The Louisville Times, shot Representative Taulbee, of Kentucky, through the head shortly before 2 o'clock yesterday afternoon. Taulbee had pulled Kincaid's nose on account of a paragraph published in The Times. It is reported that Mr. Taulbee may die. The shooting occurred at the west door of the capitol.

It was W. P. Taulbee, who represented a Kentucky district in the house during the Forty-ninth and Fiftieth Congress, who was the victim. The house was engaged in its deliberations when Kincaid's pistol shot reverberated.

The physical act of Taulbee's tweaking Kincaid's nose was considered public humiliation by Kincaid—prompting him to retaliate with a loaded revolver.

[COURTESY OF THE *KENTUCKY LEADER* ARCHIVES.]

The model room of the Patent Office is known as "Lover's Retreat" at the Interior Department, because at the lunch hour, all the flirting clerks repair to it to carry on their little schemes and designs. The cases which contain the

---

16. Ibid.

models are so thickly placed that they offer protection from prying eyes. One day, Attendant Gill, of the model-room, was passing along, when his attention was attracted by seeing a man and a girl behind one of the cases in a very compromising position.[17]

In keeping with the personality of a powerful figure, Taulbee was convinced he would rise above the snide comments and would continue his political career. On the other hand, Solomon described the public's reaction differently: "When Kincaid's article appeared, it caused a furor back home. Taulbee's political career and his marriage were soon both in ruins. He chose not to seek a third term in 1889."[18] Taulbee understandably threatened Kincaid, and according to Capitol lore, told the reporter that he had better be armed the next time they met. Angry after this public altercation, the journalist allegedly started to carry a gun.

Charles E. Kincaid was the highly respected reporter for the Louisville Times *who wrote an article critical of former representative William P. Taulbee and his supposed relationship with Patent Department clerk Laura Dodge.* [COURTESY OF THE *MAYSVILLE BUGLE* ARCHIVES.]

Solomon reported Taulbee charged Kincaid with these words: "The publication of this story has ruined me. The publication was an inappropriate intrusion into my private life." Kincaid's response to a stunned Taulbee: "I only reprinted the news that had already appeared in another publication. My paper paid me to send the news. The story was of spe-

---

17. "Lover's Retreat . . . ," *Washington (D.C.) Post*, December 1888, 1.
18. Ibid.

cial local interest. If you wish to make a statement, three columns of my paper are at your disposal."[19] Just after this conversation Solomon reported, "The strapping former Representative preferred to make his rebuttal physically. He grabbed the slight five-foot-three Kincaid and threw him against an iron bar. Though Kincaid escaped with his life, his colleagues warned him that Taulbee was still talking revenge and had begun carrying a loaded cane."[20] The next time Kincaid, who was reportedly waiting to see fellow Kentucky representative Asher G. Caruth, encountered Taulbee was on Friday, February 28, 1890, on the stairs leading to the House chamber while the House was in session.[21] Two of the Capitol doorkeepers had attempted to keep the two separated that morning. Shortly after 1:30 p.m., Taulbee and the thirty-five-year-old Kincaid met again on the east stairs where the large-boned and powerful Taulbee reportedly pulled or tweaked Kincaid's ear. All witnesses agree at that moment, Kincaid shot Taulbee once in the head, and all recounted the scene of blood gushing in a steady stream from Taulbee's mouth. The legislator's dappled bloodstains are present on the marble steps of the stairway to this day, and some believe the spirit of Taulbee still lurks, hoping to trip a member of the Fourth Estate.[22]

"Silver-tongued Taulbee Caught in Flagrante" was the headline of the 1888 article printed in the Louisville Times *which brought this accusation of Taulbee's infidelity to Kentucky citizens.*
[COURTESY OF THE *LOUISVILLE TIMES*.]

> **Kentucky's Silver -- Tongued Taulbee Caught In Flagrante**

The *Winchester Democrat* fondly described this representative as "Young, eloquent, ambitious, gifted with a superb physique,

---

19. "Lover's Retreat . . . ," *Washington (D.C.) Post.*
20. Ibid.
21. Ibid.
22. Ibid.

popular at home and admired abroad. He was a man to be envied, and his career, one to be emulated. Sprung from the people, his triumph was their victory, and illustrated the glory of a system whose genius is the equality of citizenship.[23] Taulbee had become a notable figure in Washington; tall, strong, and possessed of a powerful voice which he often used in debates with fellow congressmen. His physical attributes always gained him recognition by the Speaker whenever he chose to express his views on any measure pending, which was often."[24] Taulbee garnered friends quickly and bonded firmly with his delegation.

Born on October 22, 1851, in Morgan County, Kentucky, William Preston Taulbee was the son of former Kentucky senator William Harrison Taulbee and Mary Ann "Polly" Wilson.[25] In keeping with other early Kentucky settlers, William Harrison's parents took their young children to southern Illinois to find more suitable land and a promising life. However, his mother soon contracted miasma, commonly referred to as "swamp fever" and died. William Harrison was determined to return to eastern Kentucky and remain with his relatives. At age fourteen, he walked for several months until he found his way home. Among William Harrison and Polly's other children were several professionals: Rev. Samuel Henry Taulbee, Dr. Jackson Breckenridge Taulbee, Dr. John Andrew Taulbee, Dr. James Menifee Taulbee, Miles Kash Taulbee, Wesley (Western) Cox Taulbee, Clarinda Lane Taulbee, Mary Elizabeth Taulbee, Martha Taulbee, Eliza Burnham Taulbee, and Nancy Esther Taulbee.[26] In 1871 William Preston Taulbee

23. *Hazel Green (Ky.) Herald*, 3 April 1891, 2.

24. "The Taulbee-Kincaid Affray," *Kentucky Leader* (Lexington, Ky.), 12 March 1890, 1.

25. Ibid.; *Hazel Green (Ky.) Herald*; see also "A Distressing Affair," *Daily Capital* (Frankfort, Ky.), 1 March 1890, 2.

26. "Taulbee Family," *Early and Modern History of Wolfe County* (Borderland Books, 1972), 131; see also Rose Taulbee, *The Family Taulbee* . . . (Bloomington, Ill.: private printing), 264; see also Attorney Woodson Taulbee Wood letter to Caroline R. Miller, April 2002.

married Lou Emma Oney; taught school until 1877; was ordained as a minister while in his twenties by the Kentucky Conference of the Methodist Episcopal Church South[27]; and was later admitted to the bar in Kentucky as a lawyer.[28]

Taulbee's official residence, while he was not serving his state in Washington, D.C., was Salyersville in Magoffin County in the beautiful hills of eastern Kentucky.[29] After serving two terms, Taulbee remained away from his family and lived in Washington, D.C., as a lobbyist, real estate agent, and practicing attorney.[30] Will Press, as he was fondly called by family members, was first of all a staunch Kentucky Democrat when he was elected Magoffin County Clerk of Court in 1878 and again in 1882. He held national office from March 4, 1885, until March 3, 1889, being elected from the Tenth District in the Forty-ninth and Fiftieth Congresses. During these years Taulbee had gained national political attention at the Kentucky State Convention held in Louisville where he made a speech literally assailing the administration of President Cleveland.[31] In 1886 the *Hazel Green Herald* reported upon Taulbee's first election to a national office he was elected by voters of the district who declared themselves, "Truly we are the American people." There was only one foreign-born citizen in the entire county.[32]

Solomon's article in *The Hill* referenced this highly touted, thirty-eight-year-old Democratic politician as "Developing a reputation as one of the House's most promising new members. A tall, sinewy, six footer, Taulbee was known as 'The Mountain Orator'

---

27. "Taulbee, William Preston, 1851–1890," http://bioguide.congress.gov.

28. John E. Kleber, ed., *The Kentucky Encyclopedia* (Lexington, Ky.: University Press of Kentucky, 1992), 868.

29. "Hon. Press Taulbee Dies . . . ," *Winchester (Ky.) Democrat*, 19 March 1890, 1.

30. *Hazel Green (Ky.) Herald*, 3 April 1891, 2.

31. Ibid.; see also "Snyder Uncovers . . . ," *Kentucky Post* (Covington, Ky.), January 1983; see also "In Taulbee's Mountains," *Louisville (Ky.) Times* , 2 August 1888, 1.

32. "Truly We are the American People," *Hazel Green (Ky.) Herald*, 29 September 1886, 2.

for his roots in the eastern Kentucky hills and effective speeches on the House Floor."[33] A Frankfort correspondent for the *Daily Capital* in 1890 also reported, "Mr. Taulbee was a great favorite with the people of Eastern Kentucky. He has made considerable distinction for unusual powers as a public speaker, and for the ability with which he sustained that reputation since he entered public life. His standing in the mountain section can in nowise be better told than by the familiar phrase, 'as goes Pres Taulbee, so go the mountains.' He was endowed with a voice that was the blending of a trumpet's tone with the roar of artillery."[34] Taulbee's resonance, however, was soon silenced when he and Kincaid met on that unfortunate day.

Perhaps the first and most reliable account of the tragic events that occurred that afternoon was recorded in the *Kentucky State Journal*, published in Frankfort, Kentucky, on Saturday, March 1, 1890. This initial statement by a seemingly unbiased newspaper gave a detailed report of the shooting, as well as listing the major players and righteous characters that would have to bring forth their stories for generations to follow. The first headline read "Ex-Congressman Shot. —Attempted Assassination in the Capitol.— The Victim was W. P. Taulbee.—He Pulls the Nose of Charles E. Kincaid, a Newspaper Correspondent, and Receives a Bullet in His Head as a Reward." The article continued,

> Charles E. Kincaid, correspondent of *The Louisville Times*, shot Representative Taulbee, of Kentucky, through the head shortly before 2 o'clock yesterday afternoon. Taulbee had pulled Kincaid's nose on account of a paragraph published in *The Times*. It is reported that Mr. Taulbee may die. The shooting occurred at the west door of the Capitol.[35]

---

33. Solomon, "A Murder in the Capitol."

34. "A Distressing Affair," *Daily Capital* (Frankfort, Ky.), 1 March, 1890, 2.

35. "Ex-Congressman Shot," *Kentucky State Journal* (Frankfort, Ky.), 1 March 1890.

The House was engaged in deliberations when Kincaid's shot from his revolver reverberated through the corridors of the Capitol. The hour was about one forty and a minute later the House was almost empty, as a great crowd of distraught employees and legislators was hurrying through the corridors toward the scene of the shooting, causing utter mayhem.

Taulbee was accompanied by former doorkeeper Sam Donaldson when he was shot while coming down one of the shadow-encased stairways leading to the basement of the House wing. At this moment, Kincaid, who had recently reentered the Capitol armed with a small American double action revolver with six chambers, came down the steps behind the pair and in a hurried manner touched Taulbee on the shoulder.[36] The *Maysville Bulletin* gave the following account of what transpired next:

TAULBEE SHOT

Correspondent Kincaid Fired the Bullet.

A PATENT-OFFICE SCANDAL REVIVED

Fatal Termination of an Old Kentucky Feud.

In the late 1800s, Kentucky was quickly becoming notorious throughout the nation as a state where difficulties were not settled in a court of law but by ambushing your enemy or challenging him to a code duello.
[COURTESY OF THE *WASHINGTON CRITIC* ARCHIVES.]

> The ex-congressman wheeled sharply around, and Kincaid, raising his weapon, one of small caliber, pulled the trigger. Taulbee fell back against the wall, the blood streaming from a wound directly below his left eye. Taulbee did not appear to be badly injured. He walked in an uncertain manner down the steps, and then was assisted to the janitor's office. A great pool of blood marked the spot in the thresh hold of the doorway to this room, where Taulbee had halted for a moment.[37]

---

36. Ibid.; see also "The Kincaid-Taulbee Affair," *Kentucky Advocate* (Danville, Ky.), 7 March 1890, 1.

37. "Ex-Congressman Shot," *Kentucky State Journal*; see also Pohl, *Wicked Capitol Hill*, 27–37.

Evidently, the janitor's office was too small to allow proper attention to be administered to Taulbee, and he was taken to the room of the Committee of Public Buildings and Grounds just around the corner of the corridor. Ohio Fourth District representative T. Samuel Yoder, who was a physician, and Dr. Clarence Z. Adams, of Washington, D.C., administered emergency medical assistance.

Kincaid, meanwhile, had not attempted to get away and had reportedly leaned against the wall of the staircase utterly weakened before walking quietly away with Capitol policeman, Officer Byron.[38] Kincaid uttered, "I'm the man that did it. Not now; I'm too weak."[39] The *Maysville Bulletin* article reported Kincaid was quickly taken to the Capitol guardroom where a *United Press* reporter questioned him. He was led from the room by Officer Simon P. Mast of the Capitol police to a cab which transported him to the Twelfth Street Police Station. He was charged with assault with intent to kill.[40] Kincaid's quick reply was simply:

Chief Richard Sylvester was chief of police in Washington, D.C., in charge of the murder investigation which was reported daily in Washington, D.C., newspapers. [COURTESY OF THE METROPOLITAN POLICE DEPARTMENT OF THE DISTRICT OF COLUMBIA.]

I've just been through an attack of typhoid. Taulbee said that I am not fit to live, that I am a coward, and that I had better keep an eye on him [Taulbee]. When he came up to me this morning, he insulted me and said that I

38. "Shot in the Head," *Kentucky Leader* (Lexington, Ky.), 28 February 1890, 1.

39. "Ex-Congressman Shot," *Maysville (Ky.) Bulletin*, 6 March 1890, 1.

40. "Taulbee Dead," *Kentucky Leader* (Lexington, Ky.), 11 March 1890, 1; see also "Shot in the Head," *Kentucky Leader* (Lexington, Ky.), 28 February 1890, 1.

was a coward, and that I would not resent his insults. I told him to leave me alone or he would find out what I would do. Later he insulted me again, and I shot him.[41] When he pulled my ear today and I knew the boys on the press row had it, I was crazed.[42]

Soon after Kincaid's arrest, he was so weakened with fretful fatigue that his general physician, Dr. Harrison, was called to stay with him until late in the night.

Taulbee was laid on a chaise lounge where Dr. Yoder attended to his wounds. From there, some reports stated Taulbee was moved to his boarding house on Capitol Hill about an hour after the shooting. Dr. Adams quickly ascertained that he could not tell the seriousness of the wound, but he thought that Taulbee would recover. The transfers of Taulbee's injured body before being hospitalized at Providence Hospital,[43] simply adds to support spiritualists who frequently experience "ghost encounters" with Taulbee throughout the Capitol.

Understandably crowd reactions to the shots were reported to be typical of human inquisitiveness to ascertain the location and cause of such commotion on the east stairs. The site of Taulbee's streaming blood onto the marble halls was startling, and the witnesses' recollections and variations of the happenings were being imbedded upon their memories. Many of these same representatives and senators would have to recall these events several times within the next year while talking to correspondents, investigators, and trial lawyers. Perhaps one of the most startled eyewitnesses was a young boy who was not located for nearly two weeks before being traced by police Lieutenant Kelly and identified as Johnny Daniels. Most of the Capitol "talkers" thought it a desecration to have altercations such as this beneath the dome of the Capitol.

---

41. "Ex-Congressman Shot," *Maysville (Ky.) Bulletin,* 6 March 1890, 1.
42. Solomon, "A Murder in the Capitol."
43. "Taulbee Better," *Kentucky Leader* (Lexington, Ky.), 5 March 1890, 1.

Taulbee's blood gushed from his face and splattered on the marble stairs. These blood-stains remain to remind visitors of the violent act that members of Congress witnessed on 28 February 1890.
[COURTESY OF MARY M. WATSON.]

Even in correspondent Kincaid's local Danville, Kentucky, newspaper, *Kentucky Advocate,* the reporting of this shooting was titled with the unusual headline, "The Kincaid-Taulbee Affair," implying that the two had a long relationship which ended in tragedy for both men. The article referred to this murder as a cause of considerable excitement in the capital city, even though it was lessened when referred to as an altercation. Certainly this should not have been labeled as a simple assault, but a response to an alleged set of circumstances this particular newspaper labeled as "justifiable." This article suggested these confrontations began two years earlier when "Judge" Kincaid submitted an article for publication in the *Louisville Times* detailing the alleged disreputable act. At that time, Kincaid quickly pointed out the article had first been published in the *Post* and *National Republican* in Washington City.

Although the articles did not name Taulbee, it inferred the story was about a member of the Kentucky delegation and a Kentucky employee of the Interior Department. Kincaid felt justified, if not required, to investigate and report on the story to his readers. "A member of the Kentucky Congressional Delegation and a Kentucky belle employed in the Interior Department. I did not want all delegates besmirched, so I investigated and reported on Taulbee. It was my duty."[44] Taulbee claimed that the publication of this story ruined his political career as well as his marriage. Obviously, Mrs. Taulbee was not as apt as others to believe her husband's innocence. Rumors circulated that Representative and Mrs. Taulbee soon separated as a result of a scandalous newspaper narrative about the Patent Office clerk and Taulbee.

---

44. "Fears for Mr. Taulbee," *Washington (D.C.) Critic*, 4 March 1890, 1.

CHAPTER 3

Premature Death Reported

THE POLITICAL EDITOR OF THE *LOUISVILLE TIMES* published an article on August 10, 1888, titled "In Taulbee's Mountains," which recounted a conversation with Judge W. M. Beckner of Winchester, Kentucky. "Mr. Taulbee is not a candidate for reelection. It is understood that Taulbee had, at his former election, given a pledge not to run this time." Taulbee entered into a successful real estate business; while serving as a representative he had chaired a Committee on Real-Estate Purchases by the District of Columbia. Only two years later, the *Washington Critic*, on the day of Taulbee's death, described the persona and physique of this former representative. "In appearance Mr. Taulbee was tall and powerful, with a large-boned frame, devoid of surplus flesh. He had one of the strongest voices of any member of the House, and the tumult was never so great but that he could make himself heard above the uproar as he walked hastily down the aisle on the Democratic side and shouted to attract the attention of the speaker. He was a free talker and was on his feet taking part in debate as often as any of the younger men in Congress."[45]

The Washington scandal did the congressman no harm in the district.[46] Many in this district considered Taulbee a victim of poisonous hearsay and a bloody *code duello* often times played out in his native state. According to the *Louisville Times* article, from this point on, Taulbee repeatedly insulted and abused Kincaid even though he was offered the opportunity to clear his name in a rebuttal story.

Taulbee attempted to have Kincaid taken from the roll at the door during his first term. Clearly, Taulbee did not want him to be following his district in Kentucky daily as a reporter. Kincaid, according to Taulbee, pursued him remorselessly and would cast dispersions on all of Kentucky politicians. The men were kept apart by doorkeepers who anticipated another altercation between the two. Taulbee was often present around the House, while Kincaid's presence was lacking to the point of being quite noticeable until that particular Friday. Kincaid later recanted to a reporter, "I avoided him until I was almost ashamed at my own conduct."[47] Supposedly, Kincaid was attempting to sidestep Taulbee in the hopes that no encounter would occur, since the effects of one might adversely result in increased depression brought upon by dealing with the demands of his recently widowed and aged mother.[48]

Taulbee's room, number thirteen on the first floor of Providence Hospital, was a spacious, flower-filled room. The initial news reports of Taulbee's recovery were certainly premature. Taulbee rested well and he did not have to take opiates to sleep.

---

45. "His Assailant, Kincaid, Arrested and Much Prostrated," *Washington (D.C.) Critic*, 11 March 1890; see also http://www.jeanhounshellpeppers.com/.

46. "In Taulbee's Mountains," *Louisville (Ky.) Times,* 2 August 1888, 1.

47. John Solomon, "A Murder in the Capitol," *The Hill* (Washington, D.C.), 13 October 1999.

48. "The Kincaid-Taulbee Affair," *Kentucky Advocate* (Danville, Ky.) 7 March 1890.

Providence Hospital was located north of Folger Park in Washington, D.C. Although no longer in this building, the hospital was formerly operated by the Catholic Church and the Daughters of Charity.
[COURTESY OF THE LIBRARY OF CONGRESS ARCHIVES.]

The doctors in charge of his treatment believed unless blood poisoning set in, their patient might survive if the ball could be successfully removed. The ball originally entered the left cheek near the eye and landed between the glands of the larynx, narrowly missing cutting an artery before following a downward trajectory.[49] The belief that ex-congressman Taulbee's condition was increasingly critical was reported to all Kentuckians the following week in the *Kentucky State Journal*. At that time Taulbee's attending physicians informed the public his chances for recovery were very slight. "Pulse is becoming weaker. It is impossible for him to take food, so the end is not far off!"[50] Taulbee survived the weekend, but the next news releases quoted his physicians predicting Taulbee's death. Most reporters described his face as full of pain and sorrow, drawn and pinched with white gauze covering his forehead and one eye. These unknowing journalists classified Taulbee's condition only as a setback even though others considered him delirious and hopeless at that point.[51]

Dr. Jackson Breckenridge Taulbee remained with his brother while he was hospitalized. He witnessed the steady decline in Taulbee's condition until claimed by death on 11 March 1890.
[COURTESY OF THE *KENTUCKY LEADER* ARCHIVES.]

TAULBEE'S CONDITION.

Associated Press to THE LEADER.

WASHINGTON, Feb. 8.—There is improvement in Mr. Taulbee's condition this morning. After a refreshing sleep he is perfectly conscious. His brother, Dr. Taulbee, thinks he would be able to make a statement of the case to the District Attorney, but as the excitement attendent thereto might operate as a setback, it is not probable such a statement will be asked for today. Notwithstanding the improvement, Mr. Taulbee's condition is still critical.

---

49. "Mr. Taulbee Feverish," *Washington (D.C.) Critic*, 3 March 1890, 1.

50. "Ex-Congressman Taulbee Worse," *Kentucky State Journal* (Newport, Ky.)) 6 March 1890,1; see also "Taulbee's Condition," *Kentucky Leader* (Newport, Ky.), 9 March 1890,1.

51. "Taulbee Very Low," *Kentucky Leader* (Lexington, Ky.), 10 March 1890, 1.

The Kentucky delegation of representatives and senators visited the hospital room several times as well as other members of Congress. Speaking with Taulbee was challenging as his voice was only a whisper since his throat had to be moistened with an atomizer to prevent dryness. Seemingly, only one reporter went so far to state Taulbee's death was certain, as he was unconscious and his pulse was sporadic and much weaker. Before lapsing into delirium, Taulbee asked the doctors to locate the ball, and the surgeon intended to extract the bullet without delay. However, this procedure was promptly postponed due to Taulbee's weakening condition.[52] Former Civil War general Henry V. Boynton reported that he had some knowledge of gunshot wounds, and he believed Taulbee would recover if his doctors were not killing him with their constant probing for the ball. Further examination, with Taulbee under the influence of chloroform, revealed that at the base of Taulbee's inflamed brain near the tonsils were several small bones, which had been splintered by the bullet, giving credence that death was eminent. As a direct result of this surgical method, Taulbee lapsed into a delirious condition and had to be treated with opiates.[53] However, Dr. John W. Bayne, the physician in charge, as well as Dr. Leon L. Freidrich and Dr. Hamilton, attempted to portray a positive attitude, even while admitting Taulbee's condition was quite serious.[54] His only relief from the painful wound, for which he was given hypodermic injections, was from sleep produced by the aid of anodynes. He suffered throughout each day from the severe swelling in his throat which made swallowing even liquids quite dangerous.

One of Taulbee's brothers, Dr. Jackson Breckenridge Taulbee, who was soon in attendance at the hospital, decided Taulbee

---

52. "Taulbee Dead," *Kentucky Leader* (Lexington, Ky.), 11 March 1890, 1.

53. "Taulbee Not So Well," *Kentucky Leader* (Lexington, Ky.), 4 March 1890, 1; see also "Taulbee Dead," *Kentucky Leader* (Lexington, Ky.), 11 March 1890, 1.

54. "Taulbee Dead," *Kentucky Leader*.

should give a personal statement to the district attorney; however, a decision was made not to attempt it until more improvement was displayed.[55] Taulbee must have been considered indestructible at that time, since the *Daily Capital* described his physical constitution as "Strong, mentally and physically, with his disposition to 'pull through.' It will take more than a bullet in his face and larynx to deprive him of life."[56] The *Washington Post* reported during this week Taulbee remarked to his brother and others he thought the shooting by Kincaid was a cowardly act. Four days into his struggle, Taulbee told Dr. Yoder, with whom Taulbee had almost hourly examinations, he had never threatened Kincaid. At one point, a few days before his death, during the early morning hours, Dr. Taulbee gave an interview with members of the press who were keeping vigil on the first floor of the hospital. Dr. Taulbee's report on his brother's medical condition disclosed, "My brother is worse. I am sure he is slowly but surely sinking . . . and constantly weaker. I have no hopes. His life is fast ebbing away!"[57] Taulbee spent the last few days despondent and remarked to those around him that he accepted he was going to die.

Two days later, news reports stated his case was nearly hopeless, with only the slightest chance of recovery. Taulbee had lost a vast amount of blood immediately after the shooting and was certainly blind in one eye. Taulbee's temperature soared to 104 degrees, even with the administration of antipyretics, after he probed into the brain in search of the bullet.[58] The tract the bullet had taken twisted in such a manner keeping the wound purged was nearly impossible. Dr. Yoder stated remorsefully, "Mr. Taulbee is living mechanically. Not one chance in a hundred that he will sur-

---

55. "Taulbee's Condition," *Kentucky Leader* (Lexington, Ky.), 9 March 1890, 1.

56. *Daily Capital* (Frankfort, Ky.), 6 March 1890, 2.

57. "Slowly but Surely Sinking," *Louisville (Ky.) Courier*, 9 March 1890.

58. "Taulbee's Condition Unchanged," *Kentucky State Journal* (Newport, Ky.), 8 March 1890, 1; see also "Fears for Mr. Taulbee," *Washington (D.C.) Critic*, 4 March 1890, 1.

Representative Taulbee was treated for eleven days in a private room similar to the one pictured displaying fine Victorian furniture and lighting.
[Courtesy of the Library of Congress Archives.]

vive. I have no hope at all. . . . There is inflammation of the membrane of the brain . . . delirious all the time."[59]

Dr. Blackburn stated curtly, "I feel almost sure that the probing was overdone, to say the least. Of course, not having diagnosed the case, I cannot say whether or not the wound in itself was a fatal one. The physicians probed and probed until finally all the man's strength was gone. . . . Had he been given time to recover his strength from one probing before another was attempted, his life would have been prolonged and perhaps saved. Yes, sir, I repeat, I think the probing was overdone!"[60] In keeping with the purported sighting of Taulbee's image throughout the Capitol, it seems coin-

---

59. "The End Not Far Off," *Washington (D.C.) Critic*, 10 March 1890, 1.

cidental that the *Louisville Times* that week printed the title of their daily articles about the shooting: "The Dread Messenger Lingering by the Bedside of Mr. Taulbee Who is Likely to Receive His Chilling Touch at any Moment."[61]

Taulbee's long days of agony were terminated on Wednesday, March 12, 1890, at the Washington, D.C., Providence Hospital, where he passed away at 4:45 a.m. as a result of a shot to the head eleven days earlier. Dr. Jackson Breckenridge Taulbee; Taulbee's nineteen-year-old son, James; a brother-in-law from Salyersville, Kentucky; and a nun of the Sisters of Charity kept watch at his bedside and remained there with little sleep until the coroner pronounced him dead. Dr. Samuel Lamb, who later performed the autopsy on Taulbee, was questioned as to the condition of Taulbee's brain, what effect pressure had on the brain, and what distress had been caused by a brain abscess.[62] Furthermore, the medical abilities of the attending physicians were questioned in

TAULBEE DEAD.

FATAL TERMINATION OF THE TRAGEDY AT THE CAPITOL.

Correspondent Kincaid Rearrested on a Charge of Murder and Taken to the Police Station.

Associated Press to THE LEADER

WASHINGTON, March 11.—Ex-Representative Taulbee died at 5 o'clock this morning.

Kincaid Rearrested.

Associated Press to THE LEADER.

WASHINGTON, March 11.—As soon as the police authorities were notified of the death of Mr. Taulbee, Mr. Kincaid was rearrested and is now at the Twelfth Street police station.

"William Preston Taulbee is Dead" appeared boldly in the Frankfort, Kentucky, newspaper which revealed to readers Representative Taulbee had succumbed to inflammation which surrounded the ball fired from Kincaid's revolver. [COURTESY OF THE *KENTUCKY LEADER* ARCHIVES.]

---

60. "There was too Much Probing," *Louisville (Ky.) Times*, 13 March 1890, 1; see also "A Murder in the Capital," http://familytreemaker.genealogy.com/users/p/u/r/Sandi-I-Purol-MI/BOOK-001/0024-00.

61. "The Dread Messenger Lingering by the Bedside of Mr. Taulbee, who is Likely to Receive his Chilling Touch at any Moment," *Louisville (Ky.) Times*, 7 March 1890.

62. "Witnesses who have . . . ," *Louisville (Ky.) Times*, 2 April 1891, 1.

some newspapers, as one correspondent wrote, "Taulbee's death might not have been as a result of Kincaid's gunshot, but might have been the lack of intelligence of his attending physicians."[63] On the other hand, the doctor's opinions were respected when they asked if Taulbee made deathbed statements when he was in a lucid state; on several occasions he did make remarks as to what recourses the law should follow if he were to die.[64] When death eventually occurred, the ball had not been removed, thought to have been buried in a bone near the glands of the larynx. Reported in the *Louisville Times* that week, Dr. Cary Blackburn declared Taulbee's wound should not have brought about his death. The doctor believed the constant probing for the ball in the Taulbee's throat and not at the base of the brain displayed sheer negligence on part of the surgeon.

News of the representative's death spread rapidly on the Hill and members of the Kentucky delegation walked to the hospital to determine if Taulbee was deceased and to offer condolences to his brother and son. Reports of Taulbee's death following the most recent deliriums, and the public's curiosity about any deathbed statement generated remorseful headlines in several regional Kentucky papers, which first of all expressed regrets at Taulbee's tragic demise. Mrs. Taulbee arrived at the hospital prior to the removal of her husband's body and was able to view his

Line drawings of the shooting were printed in a regional Kentucky newspaper, clearly illustrating the position of the two men on the Capitol stairs.
[COURTESY OF THE *MAYSVILLE BUGLE* ARCHIVES.]

63. "Taulbee Dead," *Kentucky Leader* (Lexington, Ky.), 11 March 1890, 1.

64. "Kincaid's Victim," *Maysville (Ky.) Bulletin*, 13 March 1890, 1; see also "Taulbee's Condition," *Kentucky Leader* (Lexington, Ky.), 9 March 1890, 1.

remains—not attempting to attend the mandatory autopsy.

The editor of the *Daily Capital* referred to the loss of these two men: "Each of the parties to the unfortunate affair is his friend, and that sorrow or suffering should come to either gives him pain. It has been feared for a long time that the differences between the two gentlemen would lead to a sorrowful ending, bringing death, perhaps to each."[65] Within a week, this editor again wrote an article expressing the public sorrow concerning these popular men. "Wm. Preston Taulbee is dead and Charles E. Kincaid, who shot him, is in a prison cell. We have no heart to write of this tragedy. With the man who lies cold and dead, we had none but the most pleasant relations, and we mourn his death as that of one who had done, and could yet have done his state much service had his brilliant career been extended. The other—was, and is, our personal friend, and, at one time, was our close associate in newspaper work. We sorrow with him and his, as we do with the relatives of the other, so untimely cut down."[66]

65. *Daily Capital* (Frankfort, Ky.), 3 March 1890, 2.

66. "William Preston Taulbee," *Daily Capital* (Frankfort, Ky.), 12 March 1890, 1.

CHAPTER 4

Coroner's Autopsy Performed

THE DAY FOLLOWING TAULBEE'S DEATH several distinguished doctors were assisting as Dr. Lamb, of the Army and Navy Medical Museum, and Dr. Smith Townsend held a lengthy inquest. The windows of the small examination room at the rear of the Zurhorst Funeral Home at 318 Pennsylvania Avenue were draped tightly closed, blocking the view of fifty or more onlookers. The coroner's jury stood outside the house, waiting to be called inside. Once they were led in, the entrance was quite dim as there was only one gas jet for light. The awaiting casket's presence placed a pall obvious over all in attendance even before seeing the emaciated body lying prone on the examination table. In the entrance to the funeral home was the silver-ornamented coffin, covered with a black cloth which was to be the final enclosure for Taulbee's lifeless body. Sitting anxiously in that room were Taulbee's son, James, and his brother, Dr. Jackson B. Taulbee, while on the sidewalk was a policeman who kept the crowd of onlookers controlled and apart from the noticeable inquest jurors.

This group of selected jurists was comprised of William A. Peacock, Mark Hawkins, Alexander C. Lambert, John H. Hunt, James Pierce, and Clifford U. Smith. They moved inside and formed a semicircle around the table where they listened to the autopsy report and viewed the white-shrouded figure.[67] The former congressman's body had been previously laid on a board; a body exhibiting the pain and atrophy of the eleven days he held onto life. According to a shocked reporter after seeing Taulbee's stiffened form, "His limbs were scarcely more than skin and bone and the face was wan and fleshless."[68] The autopsy was to have begun at 10:30 a.m., but health officer and acting coroner Dr. Townsend had not arrived. The autopsy began at 11:00 a.m., and Dr. Lamb conducted the lengthy procedure.

Dr. Lamb initially found the entry wound to be less than the size of a lead pencil, and the swelling around his eye had nearly subsided. The dexterous surgeon guided his knife as he made sharp and decisive cuts on Taulbee's skull. In this manner the postmortem examination began in search of the bullet fired from Kincaid's pistol. Taulbee's brother relayed a message from his family to the surgeon to not disfigure the body if at all possible. The ball was eventually recovered from the center of Taulbee's brain, entering the outward corner of his left eye without much mutilation, but traveling a downward path to the base of the brain. The incision revealed his brain had been severely damaged, as well as infected from an abscess which had formed around the ball. At the completion of the autopsy, each member of the jury bent over the body and placed a light kiss, one even holding a copy of scriptures.

From this small room, the jurors and officials were moved to the Sixth Precinct Station for the inquest hearing. As noon approached, several members became hungry and one even left for

---

67. "William Preston Taulbee," *Daily Capital.*
68. "Buried in His Brain," *Washington (D.C.) Post*, 12 March 1890, 1.

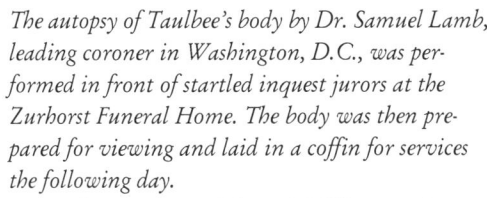

The autopsy of Taulbee's body by Dr. Samuel Lamb, leading coroner in Washington, D.C., was performed in front of startled inquest jurors at the Zurhorst Funeral Home. The body was then prepared for viewing and laid in a coffin for services the following day.
[COURTESY OF MARY M. WATSON.]

a quick sandwich. Dr. Townsend, seeing not much was going to be accomplished, excused the jury until 3:00 p.m. Inside the police station, the detectives were guarding the named assassin, while other Washington officials were working with Dr. Lamb. The medical information filed in his report gave a graphic description of the condition of Taulbee's facial wound. "The ball was located and the point of entry was determined to be below the eye in a downward trajectory and moving inward, which caused a fracture to a portion of the orbital plate. From that point, the ball moved towards the brain, fracturing and splintering a portion of the temporal bone. In fact, the ball was located in a bone and brain matter, which, if 1/16 of an inch closer, would have resulted in immediate death. Abscesses were numerous and the ménages were much inflamed and would not have allowed for any safe removal."[69]

Capital City had experienced such a tragedy and exacting autopsy only twenty-five years before when President Abraham Lincoln's head was cut apart to find the entry and intruding bullet in his brain. This autopsy report and testimony of the doctors involved in Taulbee's autopsy would be recalled a year later at the trial of Charles Kincaid. What these men did not realize in 1890 was their findings would be employed in the defense of Kincaid. In

---

69. "The Taulbee Inquest," *Kentucky Leader* (Lexington, Ky.), 13 March 1890, 2.

late afternoon, Dr. Lamb arrived and advised the jurists to go first to dinner and the inquest trial would begin about 7:00 p.m. Scheduled to appear as witnesses were Sam Donaldson (former doorkeeper at the House), Lieutenant J. W. Jones (Washington, D.C., Police), Officer Simon P. Mast (Capitol Police), Charles Christie, John Hunt (carpenter of the House of Representatives), B. H. Shriver, and John Daniels (young boy on the stairway).

Masonic services for former Congressman Taulbee were held at the Zurhorst Funeral Home at 9:40 p.m. on March 12, 1890, in Washington, D.C. Displayed on the flower draped coffin was a large pillow and cross, with an attached card reading "From a Political Friend," which expressed the sentiments of many of his fellow congressmen. The ceremonies were led by Worshipful Master Gilbert of the Knights Templar B. B. French Lodge of Masons of Washington and witnessing these rites were many national representatives and senators. In attendance was a heavily veiled Mrs. Taulbee, with two of her five sons at her side, two brothers-in-law (Dr. Jackson B. Taulbee and Dr. James A. Taulbee), and two other unnamed Taulbee brothers.[70] Taulbee's mother could not attend as it was reported in the Washington, D.C., *Evening Star* she had been driven temporarily insane as a result of the news surrounding the death of her valued son.[71] After all distinguished visi-

> **Masons Conduct the Simple Services Over the Remains of the Dead Kentuckian.**
>
> Special to the Courier-Journal.
>
> WASHINGTON, March 14.—Brief Masonic services were held last night at 9:40 o'clock over the remains of ex-Congressman Taulbee in the parlors adjoining Zurhorst's undertaking establishment. On the coffin were several exquisite floral emblems and a large pillow and cross had attached on the card. "From a political friend," and there was another large cross which came from friends at the Raymond, where Mr. Taulbee boarded for some time. A magnificent bunch of white lilies was sent by Mr. Wilson.

The Knights Templar B. B. French Association of Masons conducted brief funeral services for William P. Taulbee at 9:40 p.m. on 13 March 1890.

[COURTESY OF THE LIBRARY OF CONGRESS ARCHIVES.]

---

70. "Taken to his Kentucky Home," *Washington (D.C.) Critic*, 14 March 1890, 1.
71. "The Taulbee Tragedy," *Evening Star* (Washington, D.C.), 12 March 1890, 1.

tors and congressmen had filed by the casket, the lid was then fastened before six Masons lifted it into a waiting carriage which would carry the remains to the Pennsylvania Train Depot. From here the body and those close family members attending traveled on the Chesapeake and Ohio Railroad to Mount Sterling, Kentucky.[72] After they had arrived in a nearby village that was much more compassionate to the grieving family, Taulbee's funeral was held at 10:00 a.m., March 14, 1890, at the Hazel Green Methodist Church. His body was interred at a family burying ground at Adele in Morgan County, Kentucky.[73]

The Taulbee family name originated in France, but Stephen Taulbee and his father John Taulbee were living in Lincolnshire in England before crossing to the eastern shores of the United States in the early 1600s—settling first in Salem, Massachusetts. According to the *Massachusetts Historical Review*, in those early times women were often accused of being witches. The Taulbee family did not escape this malady as one of their members was accused of being such. Not long afterward, most of the family moved to Maryland and then to the Carolinas, where William Hitchcock Taulbee and Margaret Cannady lived before moving to Perry County, Kentucky, in 1810. Their son William Barry Taulbee married Nancy Cockerham of Rowan County, North Carolina.

William Barry and Nancy left for Illinois in 1836 with their family. One of William and Nancy's sons, William Harrison Taulbee (born June 6, 1824, in Perry County), was a young teenager at that time, but was well schooled in surviving and making his way in the wilderness. Apparently, he wandered for three years before finding his way to Hazel Green in 1842 where he was taken in and was praised for his keen skills as were a testament to his grandfather. The Taulbee progenitor served in the Revolutionary War

---

72. "Mr. Taulbee's Funeral," *Kentucky Leader* (Lexington, Ky.), 14 March 1890, 1; see also Taulbee, *Taulbee Family*, 263.

73. Kleber, *The Kentucky Encyclopedia*, 868.

This sketch of a lady dressed in Victorian funeral attire is similar to the clothing Mrs. Lou Emma Taulbee could have worn during her husband's services.
[COURTESY OF THE LIBRARY OF CONGRESS ARCHIVES.]

from the Carolinas and fought with Green and Morgan at Cow's Pen and King's Mountain. William Harrison quickly picked up reading and figuring and was a popular person, even becoming a teacher. He represented this county in the Mexican War after joining Lawrence Robinson's Third Kentucky Infantry in Lexington.

Following the war, William Harrison returned to Hazel Green and married one of the local refined women, Mary Ann "Polly" Wilson on September 20, 1848. In 1850 William Harrison and Polly settled at the headwaters of the Red River in Morgan County, where he was elected county clerk in 1858. He served in this capacity for only three years before joining Colonel John S. Williams's Fifth Kentucky Infantry fighting for the Confederacy. Before his enlistment was up, he had become a lieutenant of Com-

Kentucky senator William H. Taulbee was only a youth when he walked from southern Illinois to his grandparents' home in Kentucky. He and Mary Ann Wilson were the parents of a large family including Representative William P. Taulbee.

[COURTESY OF THE *HAZEL GREEN HERALD* ARCHIVES.]

pany A and adjutant of the entire regiment in 1862. After returning, he and Polly raised their eleven children while he taught school over a decade and was a longtime member of the emerging Christian Church. From this mountainous area he garnered enough votes to be elected in 1883 from the Thirty-fourth District to the Kentucky Senate.[74] John J. McAfee, author of *Kentucky Politicians . . .* , referred to William Harrison Taulbee as practical, but fervid; honest and earnest; and worthy of public honor and private trust.[75] The descendants of William Hitchcock Taulbee and Nancy Cockerham found themselves being pulled into politics and other occupations serving the residents of this area and the nation.

Of Representative William P. Taulbee and Lou Emma Oney's five sons, three became colonels in the military. However, there are no known descendants of these sons who carry the Taulbee name. Dr. Jackson B. Taulbee, who watched over his incapacitated

---

74. "Senator Wm. Harrison Taulbee," *Hazel Green (Ky.) Herald*, 10 March 1886, 3.

75. John J. McAfee, "Hon. William Preston Taulbee," *Kentucky Politicians: Sketches of Representative Corn-crackers and Other Miscellany* (Louisville, Ky.: Courier-Journal Job Printing Company, 1886), 149–52.

brother, contributed again to the medical field before dying in Mount Sterling at the age of sixty-seven. One of Dr. Taulbee's sons became a successful surgeon in Maysville, Kentucky, where several of his grandchildren continue to be attorneys and judges in there. Dr. John A. Taulbee's sons and daughters soon moved to Texas and their families remain in this state. Following his brother, Dr. James Menifee Taulbee's family members located in Alice, Texas. Rev. Samuel H. Taulbee's family lived for the next few generations in the Wolfe County area before migrating to Ohio. Miles Kash Taulbee continued to live out his fifty-three years in Morgan County, as well as his brother Western Cox Taulbee, who died in 1960. Of the five daughters belonging to William H. Taulbee, Nancy Esther and Clarinda Lane lived well into their eighties and are both buried near him at Insko in Morgan County. Two other daughters, Martha Roseline and Eliza Burnham, lived to their early fifties and are also interred in Morgan County. Mary Elizabeth Taulbee was born to this couple in 1865 in Morgan County, but her record of descendants ends with this information.

Taulbee's death and funeral services continued to be reported for several weeks around Kentucky, and his previous estrangement from his wife again became the topic of conversation. Their alleged separation was soon addressed clearly by Dr. Jackson B. Taulbee. He was quoted in the *Daily Capital* in regard to the varied and sensational rumors which had been circulating at times concerning the speculated divorce proceedings between his brother and his wife. Dr. Taulbee said,

> There is not, nor never has been, a word of truth in all these calumnious statements relative to the existence of even strained relations between my brother and his wife, and so far as the institution of any proceedings for divorce are concerned, that story is utterly and entirely false, and altogether unworthy of credence. And, I am in a position to know just what I am talking about. There is no man, lawyer or judge, or any body of lawyers or any court, that can come forward and truthfully state that he or they had been authorized or applied to for the

purpose of securing a divorce between my brother and his wife. ... These false, unfounded and defamatory statements which have appeared in print, derogatory as they are, both to the memory of my brother and the happiness of his widow.[76]

Dr. Jackson B. Taulbee also addressed the origin of the problems between Taulbee and Kincaid as simply a lack of job production on the part of Kincaid. Taulbee believed that Kincaid had not been performing his duties with the House doorkeeper employees and was, in fact, employing an African American worker to perform most of his responsibilities. This angered Taulbee as he believed that Kincaid was accepting his salary and only paying a portion of it to his replacement. When Kincaid could not receive the endorsement for continued employment from Taulbee and other Congressmen, Kincaid told Taulbee that he would be sorry.

Taulbee's death was greatly deplored in Eastern Kentucky and

This funeral carriage, being pulled by two cloaked horses, is similar to one used in the Washington, D.C., funeral procession of former Representative William P. Taulbee.
[COURTESY OF THE JOHN H. HENDERSON COLLECTION.]

---

76. *Daily Capital* (Frankfort, Ky.), 13 March 1890, 2.

on the day of his death, the *Washington Critic* stated, in a copy of Taulbee's biography from the *Directory of the Fiftieth Congress*, if Taulbee had lived, he certainly would have become a wealthy man. No better words befitting the slain representative were written than those by John J. McAfee, even though his compliments resonate quotes from Shakespearian literature.

> Mr. Taulbee is a brilliant speaker, and rarely fails to carry his audience with him. In presence he is tall and well-formed. His movements are at once lithe and dignified. His face is one of high intellectuality, his mouth betraying eloquence by its very formation. Mr. Taulbee is yet young, and the world is gathering honors to lay upon his shield . . . as in the days of old the men of Greece and Rome stirred the hearts of their listening countrymen with burning eloquence and valorous deeds.[77]

Most inhabitants in the high hills and wide valleys of his native state spoke positively of Taulbee's intellect and were drawn to him by his fluency of speech. Residents of this section of Kentucky were known more for their hospitality and pioneering spirit than for their ability to persuade others to vote in favor of legislation which would guide this young country into the twentieth century. However, they found within their ranks a brilliant yet common man to protect their natural resources from charlatans with connections to financiers of the East.

Dr. Taulbee expressed to those near him in the Providence Hospital room an interest in revealing the information Taulbee had relayed to him while in the hospital concerning the day of the shooting. According to Dr. Taulbee, Kincaid disclosed to Taulbee that he had no weapon, but he would retrieve one if necessary. Dr. Taulbee believed his brother attempted to avoid a renewed confrontation with Kincaid and actually invited Kincaid to go with him to a more private place to have an exchange about their perceived problems. Kincaid refused to meet with Taulbee, leaving

---

77. Ibid.; McAfee, "Hon. William Preston Taulbee," 149–52.

Taulbee with no presumed recourse but to dismiss himself from Kincaid by calling him a villain and a liar. Additionally, Dr. Taulbee admitted his brother grabbed Kincaid by the ear and directed him to the nearest door. With this accomplished, Taulbee ate lunch with members of the Kentucky delegation and returned to the House with Donaldson. During this time, Dr. Taulbee assumed Kincaid retrieved his pistol from his apartment and shortly appeared on the stairway landing. Dr. Taulbee maintained publicly his brother had no weapon of any kind on him at the time of the shooting.

CHAPTER 5

Kincaid Experienced Great Strain

THERE WAS MUCH APPREHENSION IN WASHINGTON, D.C., as to what effect this incident would have upon Charles "Judge" Kincaid, who had been laboring under a difficult strain since the unfortunate affair. Kincaid's physical and mental conditions were shattered when told of Taulbee's death. According to Solomon of *The Hill*, the first press coverage was generally compassionate toward Kincaid as clearly reported in the *New York Times*: "Mr. Kincaid passed a rather comfortable night sleeping, but little, however, owing to the severe strain which his nerves had undergone. Mr. Kincaid, under the great provocation and stinging insult, could not have done otherwise than resent it. It is, of course, unfortunate that a gentleman should have been placed into such a disagreeable and unfortunate position, being watched wherever he went by four policemen. But, nevertheless when the issue came, he had to meet it in a manly way."[78] Shortly after his arrest, Kincaid called upon Frank P. Morgan, correspondent of *Brooklyn Standard-Union*, and said, "Morgan, I wish you would send a full account of this to my newspaper, *Louisville Times*."[79] His friends believed he would not have been able to withstand a drawn-out inquest and trial, and most supporters were filled with sympathy and concern for him as noted.[80]

> Kincaid was of slight build, and an inoffensive looking man, about 35 years of age. He was formerly judge in one of the Louisville courts and his family is one of the best known in Kentucky. He has a wide acquaintance in social circles here and has spent considerable of his time in attending receptions, parties, and other society events.[81]

Kincaid to Be Indicted.

WASHINGTON, March 15.—The grand jury of the district, late yesterday evening after examining a number of witnesses, directed the district attorney to prepare an indictment against Kincaid, who shot ex Congressman Taulbee for murder.

A grand jury was empaneled to review the evidence provided by Washington, D.C., police and the prosecuting attorney. The jury's decision was Charles E. Kincaid should be tried for the murder of Representative William P. Taulbee.
[COURTESY OF *KENTUCKY STATE JOURNAL* ARCHIVES.]

Likewise, Kincaid was described in the *Maysville Bulletin* as being "a man without bitter enemies, and it was believed that Kincaid would not be charged by D.C. prosecutor Armes. There is now much sympathy for both men, although the great preponderance of sympathy is on the side of Kincaid, who has conducted himself in a very quiet and gentlemanly way since the fatal affair."[82]

---

78. John Solomon, "A Murder in the Capitol," *The Hill* (Washington, D.C.), 13 October 1999.

79. ""The Capitol Shooting," *Washington (D.C.) Critic*, 1 March 1890, 1.

80. "Ex-Congressman Taulbee," *Kentucky Advocate* (Danville, Ky.), 14 March 1890, 1.

81. "Shot in the Head," *Kentucky Leader* (Lexington, Ky.), 28 February 1890, 1.

82. "Kincaid's Victim," *Maysville (Ky.) Bulletin*, 13 March 1890, 1.

According to early reports, Kincaid was to have been kept in prison under watch of two policemen until his trial, because the murder charge was not subject to bail. Some of his friends believed several anticipated months of confinement would kill him.

Adding to the growing favorable sentiments of Kentucky newspapers, was the *Kentucky State Journal* article printed shortly after Taulbee's death—which passed quick judgment on behalf of Charles Kincaid—reporting that he did not deserve even a "pen" punishment for shooting Taulbee. Kincaid's namesake, Judge John Kincaid, was a member of the early Whig party and was considered a close friend and supporter of Henry Clay. Judge had represented his area in the state legislature and was noted for his own stature and imposing appearance. In the newspaper's editorial opinion, the aggravation that Taulbee had supposedly been inflicting upon Kincaid was sufficient to bring about the altercation. The analogy was simply put: "We'd sooner shoot a man for pulling our nose than for shooting at us. So would anyone else with the proper kind of pride."[83] Obviously law enforcement officials in Washington, D.C., did not agree with the *Kentucky Leader*, as a notice quickly appeared maintaining that Kincaid would be indicted for murder after a number of witnesses had been interviewed.[84] Begrudgingly, the *Louisville Times* explained the charges in this manner: "That, which may be regarded in Kentucky and other states of the Union as a matter of self-defense, is treated here in Washington as murder in the first degree."[85] Many in Kentucky, however, believed it was not their fashion to settle arguments in court, but to resolve it by a duel.

When the authorities were informed of Taulbee's death shortly after 6:00 a.m., Sergeant Shilling left the station and rode to Kin-

---

83. *Kentucky State Journal* (Newport Ky.), 15 March 1890, 1.

84. "Kincaid's Case," *Louisville (Ky.) Times,* 23 March 1891, 1; see also "The Kincaid Case," *Kentucky Leader* (Lexington, Ky.), 16 March 1890, 1.

85. "Taulbee Dead," *Kentucky Leader* (Lexington, Ky.), 11 March 1890, 1.

caid's apartment at 1325 F Street N.W. There, he advised Officer Oriani he would be taking Kincaid into custody. Kincaid did not delay his arrest, as he dressed quickly, realizing he would have to report again to the Twelfth Street Police Station. Although the police station was only a few blocks from his apartment, Kincaid became so despondent and weakened the police had to summon his physician to examine his condition upon arriving at the station. Kincaid was placed in a large room on the second floor with a couch and other pieces of comfortable furniture—not a typical cell where dangerous prisoners would certainly have been placed.

Soon after his incarceration, Kincaid received, through his lawyer Charles M. Smith, numerous telegram offers of bail money from prominent people in Washington, D.C., and around the nation. Proffers to become his bondsman were so abundant that any amount could have been secured, before Count Von Stamp eventually provided his surety.[86] Von Stamp considered Kincaid and himself dear friends and he offered to pay bail up to one hundred thousand dollars.[87] Information telegraphed by the Washington correspondent for the *Louisville Times* conveyed support for Kincaid when he was described as suffering greatly from mental anxiety and ill health for the year

KINCAID'S CASE.

The Selection of a Jury the First Thing In Order.

Washington, March 23.—(Special.)— Judge Hagner, who was to have tried the case of Charles E. Kincaid for the killing of ex-Congressman Taulbee, being still sick, he was not able to open his court this morning at 10 o'clock, the usual hour. It was a quarter past 11 before court convened, Judge Bradley sitting in the place of Judge Hagner. Judge Kincaid and his lawyers were on hand promptly. Judge Kincaid looked calm and collected, and sat with his attorneys just in front of the clerk's desk. His brother, Howard Kincaid, was at his side. Lists of the jurors and witnesses were called and, with a few exceptions, answered to their names

"Kincaid Case—The Selection of a Jury the First Thing in Order" was the headline used by the Louisville Times to signify the yearlong wait had ended for the Taulbee-Kincaid trial.
[COURTESY OF THE *LOUISVILLE TIMES* ARCHIVES.]

---

86. "The Kincaid-Taulbee Affair," *Kentucky Advocate* (Danville, Ky.), 7 March 1890, 1.

prior to the shooting. Kincaid, according to the report, was barely able to stand since his condition had weakened significantly while anticipating a trial in the District of Columbia. The accused was eventually released under a two-thousand-dollar bond provided by Von Stamp. His first hearing was to take place at 2:00 p.m. on the first day of March 1891, before Police Court Judge Miller. There were likewise other attorneys who offered their services to Kincaid—Col. William N. Staples of North Carolina and Judge H. Clay McKee of Mount Sterling.

Kincaid's and Taulbee's friends were one and the same with all expressing concerns for him while mourning the dead representative. At that time the city's policemen were known to be quite harsh, and Kincaid was correct in his apprehension of his future and his anticipated plea of self-defense to a charge of manslaughter—*not* murder in the first degree. Kincaid's unstable mental condition was reported by the *Kentucky Leader* with its headline, "Kincaid, a Physical Wreck," which offered more insight into his curious behavior.

> Mr. Kincaid was asleep at his boardinghouse when the police aroused him at 5 o'clock Tuesday morning and informed him of Mr. Taulbee's death. He requested to be allowed to sleep an hour longer, but the orders of the officer were peremptory, and Mr. Kincaid dressed himself immediately and was taken to the First Precinct Station, on Twelfth Street, near Pennsylvania Avenue, where he is now in custody. A reporter visited the stationhouse soon after his arrest and found Mr. Kincaid locked up in the women's cell, on the second floor, looking pale and sickly. He seemed entirely oblivious to his surroundings.
>
> Momentarily his muscles would twitch convulsively and a groan would escape his lips. The awful strain under which he has been subjected since the shooting has told terribly on him. He is a wreck of his former self. As the reporter was about to leave, the prisoner broke out in sobs and called for his mother.

87. "The Capitol Shooting," *Washington (D.C.) Critic*, 1 March 1890, 1.

The scene was touching in the extreme. Within an hour after his arrest Mr. Kincaid was so prostrated with nervous exhaustion that it was found necessary to call his regular physician, Dr. Harrison, who remained with him most of the day. Mr. Kincaid's condition is serious, and it is the opinion of many of his friends that he will not live to stand his trial.[88]

Kincaid was charged with murder and was kept under constant watch for the next week, even though no one thought he might flee the city. Nonetheless, the police instructed four or five of their detectives to watch him closely as well as the movements of other correspondents of the *Courier Journal* Bureau.[89]

✳✳✳

With the pretrial inquest investigations looming under prosecutor Armes's direction, versions of this ghastly shooting in the hallways of one of our nation's most recognizable buildings were mounting with intensity and descriptions. Most weekly newspapers throughout Kentucky were claiming to have the original and most complete description of what transpired that day. The *Maysville Bulletin* quickly released to its readers that Taulbee had seized the frail Kincaid's ear and violently jerked him backwards before shoving him against the wall where he slung insults at him. These reported physical attacks were also witnessed by those who said Taulbee had tossed Kincaid across a hallway; dashed the reporter against an iron bar; jammed his hand in the door of a streetcar; and stepped viciously on his foot in an elevator.

> **The Kincaid Trial.**
>
> WASHINGTON, April 4.—Owing to the sickness of one of the jurymen nothing was done in the Kincaid-Taulbee case yesterday morning. The court met and took a recess until 1 o'clock at which time the sick juryman had arrived, and Mr. Clagett opened the argument for the government. Mr. Clagett in his argument maintained in describing the shooting on the Capitol steps that Kincaid was guilty of murder. At 2:30 the sick juror's exhaustion compelled an adjournment for the day.

Several unfortunate illnesses led to the judge's postponing the trial several times, adding to the frustration on part of lawyers and witnesses.
[COURTESY OF THE *MAYSVILLE BULLETIN* ARCHIVES.]

---

88. "Kincaid a Physical Wreck," *Kentucky Leader* (Lexington, Ky.), 12 March 1890, 1.
89. "Taulbee Dead," *Kentucky Leader* (Lexington, Ky.), 11 March 1890, 1.

Kincaid pleaded that he was not armed, at which Taulbee supposedly told him that he should arm himself. With Kincaid's pride and manhood attacked, Kincaid was described as extremely excited and indignant. He ultimately pursued Taulbee, who had progressed toward the house restaurant steps where Kincaid found his prey. He quite frankly appeared to have snapped under the pressure of public embarrassment and reported indignities Taulbee had been heaping upon him.[90]

Barely more than a few days after Taulbee's death and autopsy, an arraignment was scheduled and a judge selected to hear the potential evidence. Kincaid's hometown newspaper was among the first to report the anticipated testimony and his appearance in the courtroom. "Mr. Kincaid came down from the jail this morning ready to plead to the indictment charging him with the murder of ex-congressman Taulbee. After a consultation, however, with prosecutor Hoge and the attorneys in the case, Mr. Kincaid was not arraigned. Following this meeting, Kincaid was allowed a light breakfast at a neighboring restaurant, before being driven back to the jail. He is looking much better than he did and getting along as well as could be expected under the circumstances."[91]

The inquest jurors reported to Chief Justice Bingham and were taken to the Zurhorst Funeral Home where they were left waiting for officials. It was soon determined that the small building would not hold all the surgeons and officials from the coroner's office, and a decision was made to move the inquest to Sixth Street Precinct Station. Kincaid did not attend the inquest as he was still being held at the Twelfth Street Station. The inquest jury was instructed they would listen to the testimony of seven witnesses. The first to make his statement was Samuel Donaldson of Tennes-

90. "The Kincaid-Taulbee Affair," *Kentucky Advocate* (Danville, Ky.), 7 March 1890, 1.

91. *Kentucky Advocate* (Danville, Ky.), 28 March 1890, 2; see also "The Kincaid Case," *Kentucky Leader* (Lexington, Ky.), 16 March 1890, 1.

see, a former doorkeeper of the House of Representatives. Donaldson's testimony was as follows:

> On the 28th day of February last, I met Mr. Taulbee, the
> deceased, near the south steps that lead down from the ladies'
> entrance to the House on the east front of the building. I had an
> engagement to meet Mr. Taulbee at that place, and had just
> heard that he was looking for me. I had been standing near the
> east entrance when I saw Mr. Taulbee coming toward me from
> the direction of the telegraph office. We met just at the top of
> the steps that lead down to the restaurant floor. Mr. Taulbee
> asked me when we met what I wanted with him. I replied: 'I
> want to see you; come and walk with me,' Taking his left arm
> on my right we walked down the first flight. We had passed
> across the first landing and had turned to the left to proceed,
> when he stopped and, turning around to me, said: 'What do
> you want with me, Sam?' I answered that I wanted to see him.
>
> At this moment, on the landing just behind us, on my right and
> on Mr. Taulbee's left, Mr. Kincaid appeared. Mr. Taulbee's face
> was turned partly toward Mr. Kincaid, when the latter said:
> 'Mr. Taulbee, you can see me now.' The deceased turned his
> face toward him when Mr. Kincaid fired the pistol shot, the ball
> taking effect just at the outside of the left eye, the blood spurt-
> ing over my hand. I turned to Mr. Kincaid and said, 'Judge, for
> God's sake don't shoot anymore.' As the ball struck him, Mr.
> Taulbee cried out, 'Oh,' and staggering in a stooping position
> down the stairs was assisted into a committee-room. Someone
> then asked who fired the shot, to which Mr. Kincaid replied, 'I
> am the man who did it.'[92]

Charles H. Christie, who was at the bottom of the stairs, also
recalled he looked up the stairs and saw a flash, but not Kincaid,
before the crowd came running out. He heard someone ask Taulbee who shot him, to which he recalled Taulbee replying, "I don't
know."[93]

---

92. "The Taulbee Inquest," *Kentucky Leader* (Lexington, Ky.), 13 March 1890, 2; see
also Richard Sylvester, "Kincaid-Taulbee Tragedy," *District of Columbia Police: A Retrospect of the Police Organizations* (Washington, D.C.: Gibson Brothers, 1894), 237–38.

The youngest witness was called to testify what he remembered from the day in question. Johnny Daniels stated he was stepping down the stairs and heard a disturbance between two men who were near the base of the stairs. Daniels added that he saw another witness, who was not in court that day—a "colored" man who soon disappeared from his view. Upon hearing a shot fired below him, Daniels ran in another direction, but not before he saw Kincaid with a gun in his hand, pointing in an upward direction as if he might fire again, and shouting, "I did it!"[94]

Most, a Capitol policeman, who was on the basement floor of the House side of the Capitol, provided the most damaging testimony to Kincaid. When he heard the shot, he hurried to the spot of the altercation in time to hear Kincaid (who was only four to six feet away) reply he had fired the weapon. Policeman Most then took the pistol from Kincaid and placed him under arrest. According to J. B. Donnelly, who was also near the spot of the shooting, Kincaid admitted to the killing, stating that Taulbee had assaulted him that morning, by seizing him by the lapel of his coat, and calling him a liar. Varying testimony was heard next by the court

Most essential witnesses were recalled by the defense and prosecution, particularly coroner Dr. Samuel Lamb and one of Taulbee's attending physicians, Dr. J. W. Bayne.
[COURTESY OF THE *LOUISVILLE TIMES* ARCHIVES.]

MORE WITNESSES EXAMINED.

The Day's Proceedings of the Kincaid Murder Trial.

WASHINGTON, March 27.—The trial of Charles E. Kincaid for killing ex-Congressman Taulbee, of Kentucky, was continued in the criminal court yesterday. William McCormick, an assistant doorkeeper of the house of representatives, testified to the trouble that occurred between Taulbee and Kincaid just before the shooting occurred. Witness said that Taulbee told Kincaid that he wanted to see him. Kincaid replied that he did not wish to see Taulbee. Taulbee repeated that he wanted to see Kincaid. Kincaid replied: "Well, you see me now." Taulbee then took Kincaid by the lapel of his coat and gave him a pull and exclaimed: "Come out here." Kincaid replied that he would not go and did not wish to talk with Taulbee.

---

93. "The Taulbee Inquest," *Kentucky Leader* (Lexington, Ky.), 13 March 1890, 2.

94. "The Taulbee Tragedy," *Evening Star* (Washington, D.C.), 12 March 1890, 5.

when Mr. Robert Woodbridge, an assistant doorkeeper, reported to have seen Taulbee pull Kincaid's ear.[95] The inquest ended with the jury's verdict: "Taulbee came to his death from the pistol wound, the pistol being held in the hand of Charles E. Kincaid, in the U.S. Capitol building, on February 29, 1890."[96] Kincaid was charged on one count of felonious assault with a pistol, valued at five dollars, held in his right hand and fired at Taulbee, eventually causing his death.

---

95. "Pulled His Ear," *Kentucky Leader* (Lexington, Ky.), 26 March 1891, 1.
96. "The Taulbee Inquest," *Kentucky Leader* (Lexington, Ky.), 13 March 1890, 2.

CHAPTER 6

Public's Accusations Remained

The Taulbee-Kincaid difficulty must not have been the only disruption in the political climate during the late nineteenth century. Speaker Thomas B. Reed of Maine, the "disappearing quorum" sponsor in 1890, sent a letter which was published in the *Kentucky Leader* to diplomat George W. Caruth of Kentucky. The correspondence revealed great anxiety and apprehension of such tragedies that might occur, even to himself. Speaker Reed's words were written just before the Taulbee shooting and explained his fear of coming to Kentucky as he thought he would be killed. In the letter he wrote, "Such events occur much too often. I think I can make more by dying later and elsewhere."[97] Caruth had grounds for his apprehension as nearly three decades earlier a well-known correspondent, Luther R. Dobyns of the *Louisville Times*, carried out a public battle with Richard Collins, editor of the *Maysville Eagle*. This feud lasted until Dobyns threatened Collins

---

97. "Don't Want to Die," *Kentucky Leader* (Lexington, Ky.), 2 March 1890; see also "Caruth, George William," *The National Cyclopaedia* (New York: James T. White and Co., 1910), 176.

with a cowhide whipping if Collins did not publish a retraction of the charges Dobyns had participated in a swindling operation in Maysville. On Friday evening, December 27, 1853, Dobyns approached Collins on a Maysville street, and Dobyns fell to the ground, mortally wounded.[98] Another more famous dispute developed during the year of the Kincaid–Taulbee debacle; the infamous Devil Anse Hatfield–Ranell McCoy dispute in Kentucky and West Virginia which was portrayed on front pages of daily newspaper accounts across the nation in 1888.[99] Modern-day films have catapulted this violent feud onto television as a 2012 miniseries.

This short-lived Taulbee–Kincaid feud has been recorded in a song which has been accompanied by an interview with Taulbee's great-granddaughter, Virginia Burton. The words and accompaniment were both compiled by Jeni Hankins and Billy Kemp.

Silver Tongued Taulbee and Charlie Kincaid

The knock at her door came as a surprise.
Your husband's been shot, there's a good chance he's died.
So she packed up five children—her widow's journey begun—
to say goodbye to Daddy—the once Congressman.

Chorus:

Where is the witness can say it was murder?
Who can read the stain on the marble stairs?
'Can you see me now?' Kincaid whispered.
And a shot rang out in the cold winter air.

Silver-tongued Taulbee was his name to his back.
A reporter's slander knocked his star off track
'With the brown-haired Miss Dodge in the Patent model room,'
said the *Louisville Times* and the rumors they grew.

The reporter, Kincaid, was sickly and short.
He held a grudge against Taulbee—the tall, handsome sort.
Something of a bully, Taulbee tweaked Kincaid's nose
in the House Chamber where all Washington still goes.

---

98. "Yesterday's News," *The Kentucky Register* 95, no. 1 (Winter 1997): 56.

99. John E. Kleber, "Hatfield-McCoy Feud," *The Kentucky Encyclopedia* (Lexington, Ky.: University Press of Kentucky, 1992), 418.; see also Roy Helton, "Old Christmas," *Lonesome Water* (New York: Harper and Brothers, Publishers, Inc.), 1930.

Kincaid went home for his pistol (the deed good as done)
to repay Taulbee for his moment of fun.
Down came Taulbee, down the Capitol stairs,
but he was stopped by a bullet that greeted him there.

During the following months, Representative Taulbee's memory was allowed to "rest in peace" in Kentucky, before the horrible accounts of his shooting surfaced this time in a court of law.

The name Taulbee did emerge once more before the turn of the century, but this time as a personality in the poem, "Old Christmas," by Roy Helton of Washington, D.C. Taulbee's image was specifically characterized to include a murder plot in which a character named Taulbe Barton[100] [Taulbee] killed a woman's husband, and she, in turn, killed Taulbe, leaving the reader to assume that Sally Anne Barton was talking to the ghost of Lomey Carter. This poem has been included in several high school literature series as an example of a modern Appalachian ballad. Helton, a blind poet, knew firsthand the reputation of Representative Taulbee during the time that Helton's father, Dr. Addison S. Helton of Kentucky, was a medical student in Washington and later

DON'T WANT TO DIE

Speaker Reed's Letter Declining an Invitation to the Bluegrass Club Dinner at Louisville.

Associated Press to THE LEADER.

WASHINGTON, March 1.—Just before the Taulbee shooting affair at the Capital yesterday, speaker Reed showed to Representative Stewart, of Vermont, a letter he had just written to Mr. Caruth, of Kentucky, which is too good to keep private. Mr. Stewart gave its contents to several colleagues, through whom it in turn reached the press, to the discomfiture of the Speaker. The letter reads as follows:

OFFICE OF SERGENT-AT-ARMS.
HOUSE OF REPRESENTATIVES,
WASHINGTON, Feb. 28.

Dear Mr. Caruth:

I shall not accept the invitation tendered me by the Bluegrass Club. The reason is very simple. I notice that Jay F. Durham is president. Now Jay F. Durham assured me during the late "Disturbances" that if they had me in Kentucky they would kill me. Knowing the said Durham to be a journalist, his declarations to me impart absolute verity. I do not wish to be killed, especially in Kentucky, where such an event is too common to attract attention. For a good man to die anywhere is, of course, a gain; but I think I can make more by dying later and elsewhere.

This letter, written by Representative Thomas B. Reed of Maine shortly after the shooting of former representative Taulbee, was recalled by visitors to the trial and residents of Kentucky. Representative Reed chose not to attend dinner in Kentucky after hearing about various duels, which always left one person dead. [COURTESY OF THE DAILY CAPITAL ARCHIVES.]

---

100. Roy Helton, "Old Christmas," *Adventures in Appreciation, Vol. 4* (San Diego, Calif.: Harcourt, Brace, 1958).

Roy Helton was a young poet who living in Washington, D.C., where his father was a doctor. Among Helton's countless poems centering on the Appalachian Mountain area was "Old Christmas Morning," which relates a dramatic story of murderers and spirits who walked the hills on that particular day, including one named "Taulbe."
[COURTESY OF MARY M. WATSON.]

practiced in the city when Taulbee was killed. Undoubtedly, this fictionalized account of a "Taulbe" murder kept this tragic event in the minds of young readers throughout the next century.

Old Christmas Morning

Where you coming from, Lomey Carter,
So airly over the snow?
And what's them pretties you got in your hand?
And where you aiming to go?

Step in, Honey. Old Christmas morning
I ain't got nothing much.
Maybe a bite of sweetness and corn bread,
A little ham meat and such.

But come in, Honey! Sally Anne Barton's
Hungering after your face.
Wait till I light my candle up.
Set down! There's your old place.

Now, where you been so airly this morning?
Graveyard, Sally Anne.
Up by the trace in the salt lick meadows
Where Taulbe Kilt my man.

Taulbe ain't to home this morning. . .
I can't scratch up a light.
Dampness gets on the heads of the matches,
But I'll blow up the embers bright.

Needn't trouble. I won't be stopping.
Going a long ways still.
You didn't see nothing, Lomey Carter,
Up on the graveyard hill?

Yes, elder bushes, they bloom, Old Christmas,
And critters kneel down in their straw.
Anything else up in the graveyard?
One thing more I saw.

I saw my man with his head all bleeding
Where Taulbe's shot went through."
What did he say? He stooped and kissed me.
What did he say to you?

Said, Lord Jesus forgive your Taulbe,
But he told me another word.
He said it soft when he stooped and kissed me.
That were the last I heard.

Taulbe ain't to home this morning.
I know that, Sally Anne,
For I kilt him, coming down through the meadow,
Where Taulbe kilt my man.

I met him upon the meadow trace
When the moon were fainting fast.
And, I had my dead man's rifle gun
And kilt him as he come past.

But, I heard two shots. T'was his was second.
He shot me 'fore he died.
You'll find us at daybreak, Sally Anne Barton.
I'm laying there dead at his side.[101]

Taulbee's coffin was placed on a train in Washington, D.C., and taken to West Liberty,
Kentucky, where it was removed to a statecoach for its final journey to the family cemetery.
[COURTESY OF THE LIBRARY OF CONGRESS ARCHIVES.]

---

101. Roy Helton, "Old Christmas Morning," http://www.tnellen.com/cybereng/
poetry/poems/old_christmas_morning.html.

CHAPTER 7

Circuit Court Trial Conducted

THE TRIAL DATE WAS SET ON MARCH 3, 1891, in Washington, D.C., for Charles E. Kincaid, the accused murderer of the former congressman William P. Taulbee. Interest in this case had not waned in the intervening months and the attention of a lengthy trial was now reaching high repute. This prosecution was considered so important in the Commonwealth of Kentucky that the *Louisville Times* devoted a section daily on its front page to recount the entertaining details. Judge Alexander B. Hagner was the first judge assigned the difficult case, and not even he was able to start this trial in a timely manner since he was quite ill.[102] The trial was rescheduled from March 3, 1891, since Congress was in session and because attorney Daniel Voorhees was experiencing rheumatic fever. Judge Andrew C. Bradley at long last convened the court at 11:15 p.m., Monday, March 23, 1891, with Kincaid and his lawyers present. The chief prosecutors were Charles C. Cole and Howard

---

102. "The Kincaid Trial," *Hazel Green (Ky.) Herald* , 27 March 1891, 2.

C. Clagett, while Bradley served as trial judge. Prosecutor Cole had just recently been appointed by President Benjamin Harrison three weeks prior and this was his first major trial.

Several judges presided over an assortment of pretrial hearings: Edward F. Bingham, Alexander B. Hagner, and Martin V. Montgomery. The beginning of this trial signified the end of the lives of two of Kentucky's rising megastars in public life—a noted congressman and an exceptional newsman, who first worked as a private secretary to Senator John Williams, before becoming a correspondent in Washington, D.C., for several national newspapers. Kincaid had to plead not guilty to the charges, and the selection of the jury followed with seven seated before the noon recess.[103]

Kincaid was described as calm while seated with his brother, Howard Kincaid, at his side. Immediately after calling the role of potential jurors, the counsel

WELL DEFENDED.

Judge Kincaid's Case Managed With Ability and Strongly Made Out.

Washington, April 3.—(Special.)—Gen. Grosvenor has gone to Ohio, being obliged to go at once to his home at Athens, where he is to conduct a homicide case. He made a great reputation here in the Kincaid case as one of the attorneys for the defendant, and for the past two weeks or more has given his undivided attention to the matter. It is very much regretted here that Gen. Grosvenor is not to address the jury at the closing of the case. Gen. Grosvenor, however, made the presentation speech for the defense last week, and greatly impressed the jury.

"Well Defended" was the reaction of Louisville, Kentucky, citizens who believed in the innocence of correspondent Charles E. Kincaid. Ohio general Charles H. Grosvenor delivered the majority of the closing statements by the defense but was unable to attend the closing day of the trial.

[COURTESY OF THE *LOUISVILLE TIMES* ARCHIVES.]

for Kincaid asked to withdraw the plea of not guilty and requested to file a motion to quash the indictment *pro forma*, but was overruled.[104] The chief defense lawyer was three-term Ohio representative Charles H. Grosvenor, and his assistants in the pretrial

---

103. "Kincaid's Plea," *Kentucky State Journal* (Newport, Ky.), 24 March 1891, 1.

104. "Kincaid's Case," *Louisville (Ky.) Times*, 23 March 1891, 1.

research were C. Maurice Smith, former Indiana judge; Congressman Jeremiah M. Wilson; and Senator Daniel W. Voorhees of Indiana. The process came to an even slower pace the next morning
after several potential jurors stated they had previously formed
opinions and could not be swayed by any testimony.[105] At the
day's end, a jury consisting of eight white men and four African
American men was seated.[106] Although a year had passed since the
murder incident, the obvious sensationalism and coverage of this
case remained clear in the minds of the citizens in the nation's capital.

Among more than fifty witnesses, who had traveled great dis-
tances from Massachusetts to Louisiana, were several representatives and governors who presented their statements to the court.[107]
The first individual to take the stand was James W. Jones, a Capitol

*Charles E. Kincaid used a weapon similar to this American double action revolver to shoot
former representative Taulbee on the Capitol stairs.*
[COURTESY OF THE H & R FIREARMS COLLECTION.]

105. "Getting a Jury," *Louisville (Ky.) Times*, 24 March 1891, 1.
106. "Judge Kincaid's Trial," *Kentucky Advocate* (Danville, Ky.), 27 March 1891, 1.
107. Ibid.; "Kincaid's Case."

policeman, who testified that before hearing the pistol shot, he was proceeding up the stairs when he observed Taulbee and Donaldson on the first landing. When Jones demanded information from Kincaid, he replied that Taulbee had indeed pulled his ear and Jones proceeded to examine it, finding it red and swollen. Following his testimony were the words from another Capitol policeman, B. F. Graham, who began the blood-smattering narrative of the first of frequent moves of the injured Taulbee from the steps, to the janitor's closet, and finally to a committee room. Perhaps the most tangible incriminating evidence produced from these policemen was the description of the lightweight overcoat worn by Kincaid which could have been an excellent method to conceal a pistol.[108]

At the insistence of the prosecution, the next witness was Henry W. Brewer, a civil engineer, who produced a large diagram of the steps and corridor of the Capitol building. This drawing was exhibited on the wall of the courtroom so all jury members could ascertain the exact locations of the men involved. Donaldson was called next on behalf of the prosecution. He testified that he had seen Taulbee on the day of the shooting first in the hall, later in the House restaurant, in the corridor, and finally on the steps to the landing. Donaldson reported Taulbee asked him, "What do you want, Sam?" Donaldson remembered replying, "I want to see you. Come with me." Still on the landing, Donaldson reported he and Taulbee heard someone call to them from the landing above: "Taulbee, you can see me now." Taulbee, according to Donaldson, turned his head in that direction and saw Kincaid draw his gun before Taulbee started toward Kincaid then stopped a little more than an arm's length. There was an immediate flash of a pistol. Instantly Donaldson pleaded with Kincaid, who was standing not five feet away, to not shoot again. Donaldson's description of the next few moments of bedlam was recounted carefully for the jury

---

108. "Proceedings in the Kincaid Case Progressing Somewhat Slowly," *Louisville (Ky.) Times*, 25 March 1891, 1.

including the movements from Taulbee's grabbing his wounded face to his stumbling down the steps. By this time, Donaldson recalled that quite a crowd had gathered in the corridor and someone shouted out, "Who shot this man?" "I shot him. He wounded me this morning," retorted Kincaid.[109]

With this testimony for the prosecution concluding, the defense attorneys called the shooting a simple act of revenge. Chief defense lawyer, General Grosvenor, demanded to know from Donaldson what his business had been with Taulbee that morning and the reason he had been in the Capitol. Donaldson finally admitted he was attempting to have the threatening difficulty avoided between Taulbee and Kincaid. Donaldson also acknowledged he knew a potential witness, Miss Millmore, who boarded at the same residence with him. He testified initially that he had not informed Millmore that Taulbee had told Kincaid to arm himself as he intended to kill him. Donaldson was pinned down closely on these points, and he insisted if he had told Miss Millmore anything of this nature, it was hearsay and not of his own knowledge. Donaldson also denied he said to Miss Millmore at the boarding house the night of the shooting he had been trying all day to keep Taulbee away from Kincaid.

The *Kentucky State Journal* also reported the testimony that

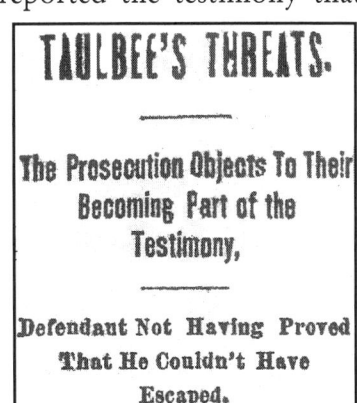

Defense attorneys for Charles E. Kincaid fought vigorously for Taulbee's public threats to be included in the testimony for the jurors to hear. These threats were voiced to Kincaid throughout the two years prior to the shooting. Conversely, the prosecution acted to prove that Kincaid had ample time and ability to leave.

[COURTESY OF THE *LOUISVILLE TIMES* ARCHIVES.]

TAULBEE'S THREATS.

The Prosecution Objects To Their Becoming Part of the Testimony,

Defendant Not Having Proved That He Couldn't Have Escaped.

---

109. "Hearing Evidence." *Louisville (Ky.) Times*, 25 March 1891,1.

transpired with its characterizing headline "Kincaid's Trial—It is Finally Begun in Washington City—Sensational Story of How Taulbee Was Shot Related by an Eye Witness—Samuel Donaldson, Formerly Door-keeper of the House Who was With the Murdered Man at the Time of His Death." After giving his disturbing testimony, Donaldson was accused of threatening to color his testimony, personally hoping that Kincaid would be convicted. The only additional news Donaldson revealed at this time was that he witnessed Representatives Charles A. Bontelle, John G. Carlisle, and James Brown of Indiana at the front of the stairs immediately after the murder.[110]

Another witness, Frank P. Lovel of Boston, was called by chief prosecutors Charles C. Cole and Howard C. Clagett, to bring forth interesting facts to support the description of general mayhem in the Capitol that day. Lovel stated he had no prior personal relationship with Taulbee; therefore his testimony should not be suspect. He distinctly testified he saw Kincaid clutching the smoldering pistol directly after hearing the shot, but Lovel placed the shooting on the steps at a different location than Donaldson. This explicit description gave the defense attorneys a great deal of controversy to digest. Furthermore, Lovel described the revolver being held by Kincaid as smoking and represented Kincaid as saying he shot Taulbee because he insulted him that morning. Lovel pointed directly at Kincaid sitting in the court and correctly identified the assailant.[111]

A differing news article on a more regional scale stated this murder in fact had attracted statewide press coverage. The *Maysville Bulletin,* during the early days of the trial which lasted from March 23 to April 8, 1891, used this heading to catch the readership's interest: "It Will Be Begun Today and Will Attract

---

110. "Kincaid's Trial," *Kentucky State Journal* (Newport, Ky.), 26 March 1891, 1.
111. Ibid.

Widespread Attention." Adding to the demand for those seeking "tidbits" of juicy gossip was the referencing of the original article about Taulbee's alleged affair, even though it had occurred nearly three years earlier. The *Bulletin* article stated the account of this tryst had appeared in a morning newspaper in Washington, D.C., and, as it concerned Kentucky people, Kincaid felt compelled to release it to more readers. He not only dispatched it to the *Louisville Times*, an afternoon paper, but also to the *New York Morning Journal*, one of the papers wiring him for the story.[112]

Corroborating the testimonies given by Donaldson and Lovel was J. B. Donnelly, who testified he heard Kincaid say several times he was the assailant. When asked to repeat the word "assailant," Donnelly repeated that he heard Kincaid use that exact word. However, the next witness, Reuben E. McCormick, a doorkeeper at the east door of the House of Representatives, testified it was Taulbee who first asked to see Kincaid, with Kincaid replying he did not want to see him. With that exchange of words, McCormick reported Taulbee took hold of the lapel of Kincaid's coat and pulled him, saying, "You're a liar." At this point the testimony of several witnesses differs markedly, with McCormick maintaining Taulbee returned to the hall and Kincaid walked off down the corridor, but soon returned to the east door and talked with McCormick himself. Kincaid was so bold as to ask McCormick what he would do in this case of difficulty with Taulbee as he was not able to cope with such a man. Most of McCormick's testimony was corroborated by another doorkeeper Robert Woodbridge, especially the testimony concerning the report of the weapon resounding through the marble clad halls.[113]

Jay Dunham, a Washington correspondent, was perhaps the strongest witness on Kincaid's behalf. Dunham testified he was an

---

112. *Maysville (Ky.) Bulletin*, 26 March 1891, 1.

113. "The Taulbee Case: Examination of Witnesses Began in Washington Yesterday," *The Arizona Republican* 2, no. 120 (27 March 1891).

This newspaper headline expressed the compassion emitted by all who knew both Taulbee and Kincaid. The disagreement between the two culminated in a shooting in one of our nation's most revered buildings, leaving permanent stains both on the marble and in the minds of citizens who supported each man.

[COURTESY OF THE *LOUISVILLE TIMES* ARCHIVES.]

SETTLED A GRUDGE.

Two Kentuckians Meet at the National Capitol.

ONE IS QUITE LIKELY TO DIE.

Ex-Congressman Taulbee Shot by Correspondent Kincaid.

BLOOD ON THE WHITE MARBLE.

Ending of a Little Quarrel That Has Been of Long Standing.

SYMPATHY DIVIDED BETWEEN THE TWO.

observer to many embarrassing threats made by Taulbee against his friend Kincaid stating Taulbee had insulted Kincaid at least a half a dozen times before the shooting.[114] Kincaid admitted to Dunham he was sick and weak and not armed, even with a cane. When Kincaid left for a few minutes, he returned with his cane as he stepped to the stairway, all within the obvious sight of McCormick.[115]

Doorkeeper Woodbridge testified he also heard this particular conversation between Kincaid and Taulbee, which Woodbridge described as occurring in low tones, but was able to hear every word. His version was Kincaid told Taulbee he could not cope with him physically, and Taulbee returned with his impudent statement, "You are a liar!" Woodbridge also testified that Taulbee pulled Kincaid's ear with his left hand, in fact Kincaid's right ear.[116] Woodbridge overheard Kincaid admitting when he saw

---

114. "Murder—Taulbee Shot," *Washington (D.C.) Critic*, 28 February 1890, 1.

115. "Hearing Evidence," *Louisville (Ky.) Times*, 26 March 1891, 1.

116. Ibid.

Taulbee put his hand in his pistol pocket, he decided to fire his own weapon.[117] One of the subsequent witnesses, who was questioned at length about Taulbee's lingering death, was Dr. Bayne, who reported on one occasion near Taulbee's demise, he spoke with the dying former representative, Dr. Jackson B. Taulbee, and James Taulbee, the son of the now deceased. They all agreed Taulbee was cognizant and capable of reasoning in regards to his statements until the eighth of March, when Taulbee's mind began to wander, as a result of inflammation in the brain.

When the wounded Taulbee and his brother were reviewing a previously written statement, Dr. Bayne testified Taulbee was capable of understanding his words on that day, but Taulbee was unable to give a statement to Assistant District Attorney Armes only a few days later. Dr. James B. Taulbee next took the stand to identify the statement made on March 8 by his dying brother. He stated he believed from their first hospital meeting Taulbee would not live as a result of being shot, and he repeated this thought to his brother, after being asked to speak candidly about his condition.[118] Taulbee's only accounting of the attack was brought into testimony, "I did not know Kincaid was near and did not know who it was who shot me until I was told."

Since the defense was attempting to prove Kincaid feared for his life, witness William A Stillman, a farmer from Friendship, New York, was called[119] to relate his version of the events of that day. Stillman stated he was not personally acquainted with Taulbee, but on that day happened to be in Washington at the Capitol. Stillman testified he heard Taulbee speak at Friendship during the presidential campaign of 1888, and he did recognize Taulbee standing in the Capitol with another man near the stairway. He recol-

---

117. Ibid.; "Murder—Taulbee Shot."

118. "Taulbee's Statement," *Louisville (Ky.) Times,* 26 March 1891, 1.

119. Mark Thornton, "Charles Kincaid Trial: 1891," Great American Trials 2002, Encyclopedia.com.18 February 2013 < http://www.encyclopedia.com >.

lected the words spoken between Taulbee and Kincaid to be "Keep off!" or "Keep Back!" Stillman stated he looked up and saw Taulbee advancing and in the act of reaching out.

Even after the district attorney vigorously cross examined Stillman, he appeared to be unshaken with his testimony. He also reported he attempted to flee from the Capitol, fearing a volley of shots, and admitted he was excited and anxious—the appearance he also gave during his questioning. The testimony of Stillman was questionable because he had been called as a potential witness only a month before the start of the trial. The judge did get this witness to reveal that his health had been poor for almost twenty years, therefore, he was not considered as a *bona fide* witness by the prosecution.[120]

120. "Saw the Shooting," *Louisville (Ky.) Times*, 28 March 1891, 1.

CHAPTER 8

Trial Reached Conclusion

WITH THE TRIAL CONTINUING INTO ITS SECOND WEEK and after a myriad of witnesses appearing, Defense Attorney Grosvenor's statement to the jury spoke words of self-defense on behalf of Kincaid. Kincaid perceived Taulbee to be charging him. Since he was weak and was not of a size to deal with him, Kincaid removed the revolver hidden in his coat. He pulled the hammer on his revolver and fired. Grosvenor stated even though Taulbee was shot squarely in the face, Kincaid did not perceive him to be dangerously wounded; and he did not attempt to shoot again. Doorkeeper Woodbridge's testimony was again brought forth for discussion in regard to other witnesses' accusations that Taulbee ordered Kincaid to arm himself.

Perhaps the most damaging testimony to the prosecution was the judge's allowing the defense attorney to enter Dr. Harrison's testimony regarding the health of Kincaid over the previous five years. His words were in regard to Kincaid's defective eyesight, but Judge Bradley retorted, "Kincaid's sight must be pretty good since he was able to hit Taulbee with his shot." Reiterating this account was the *Louisville Times* caption for that evening's paper, which read, "Judge Bradley Refutes All Efforts to Show State of Defendant's Health." Dr. Harrison was allowed to testify he first treated Kincaid in 1885 but was not able to give any further information due to objections. His only statement allowed was he had operated on Kincaid's eye in a previous year for a tumor on the eyelid.[121] Another defense witness, a newspaper correspondent, was called and offered Kincaid was a very feeble man at the time of the shooting and his reputation was good in every respect.[122]

On this particular trial day, an unusually large number of spectators were in the courtroom when the trial resumed. Most in attendance anticipated Judge Bradley would decide whether testimony regarding the alleged threat made against the life of Kincaid by Taulbee should be admitted. Bradley allowed this testimony which was a triumph for the defense, as many more witnesses were now allowed to speak. E. W. Kelly, of Terre Haute, Indiana, testified he was well acquainted with Taul-

Violent feuds in Kentucky were becoming all too frequent in the decades following the duel between Union general "Bull" Nelson and Confederate general Jefferson C. Davis. The Hatfield and McCoy feud was the longest and perhaps most recalled grudge throughout eastern Kentucky.
[COURTESY OF THE *WASHINGTON CRITIC* ARCHIVES.]

121. "Self-Defense," *Louisville (Ky.) Times*, 27 March 1891, 1.
122. "So Spoke the Slain," *Louisville (Ky.) Times*, 30 March 1891, 1.

bee, and within a week after the publications concerning Taulbee, he frequently made threats against Kincaid. The prosecuting attorney objected to these statements but they were permitted, and Kelly disclosed he had told Kincaid that Taulbee wanted to kill him. In fact, Kelly alleged Taulbee once remarked, "I intend to kill Kincaid. The world is not big enough for him to escape my vengeance." Kelly went so far as to warn Kincaid, while the two were in the office of the *Cincinnati Enquirer*, he had better be at his guard, as Taulbee would injure him. Kelly ultimately had to admit he had never noticed Taulbee with a pistol.

Another correspondent, Col. Perry S. Heath, of the *Indianapolis Journal*, testified about a week before the shooting he was in the reporters' room behind the House Press Gallery, when Taulbee entered and began to talk about a certain disturbing publication. Taulbee said he believed the troubling stories would not have been

Inside the Capitol is this grand stairway on which hundreds of representatives and senators travel to their offices where they craft the laws of our nation. On other stairs in the Capitol, there remain bloodstained steps which, reportedly, await a reporter to stop and remark as to their origin.
[COURTESY OF LIBRARY OF CONGRESS ARCHIVES.]

published but for Kincaid, and he intended to cut his throat. Heath also stated he had consulted with Taulbee six weeks before the shooting and again pleaded with him to end the controversy. Following his startling statement, came another damning testimony from former Kentucky congressman Polk Laffoon stating he did know of the difficulty between the two men. As a result of the publication concerning the relationship, if any, between Taulbee and Miss Holland, Laffoon, Taulbee's personal friend, was interested in smoothing over the difficulty. Laffoon admitted under oath Taulbee repeatedly said he intended to kill Kincaid, and Laffoon advised him against it.[123]

The last week of the trial began with conflicting testimony when the first witness, Engineer Edward C. Stubbs, was asked if he knew if Taulbee carried a gun in the summer of 1886. However, this questioning was overruled. One of the last witnesses, Mr. Curtis, was recalled and was allowed to state he believed Kincaid to have been of admirable character. Furthermore, he had never heard any threats from Taulbee in regard to Kincaid that had been heard by other witnesses, but he did admit Kincaid was extremely agitated—his face flushed, then pale on the day of the shooting. Next called was newspaper correspondent William B. Shaw who reportedly knew Kincaid to be a man of excellent general reputation, and repeated he had heard others mention threats by Taulbee, in particular Senator Joseph C. S. Blackburn, but this conversation occurred a year before the shooting. Another congressman, Representative James B. McCreary from Kentucky, testified Taulbee was a strong, active, and muscular man, unlike the spindly Kincaid. He also affirmed he had known Kincaid for fifteen or twenty years, and was well acquainted with his family. As a former governor of Kentucky, McCreary had appointed Kincaid a judge of the court at Lawrenceburg, Kentucky, where he enjoyed a splendid reputa-

---

123. Ibid.

tion—socially, politically, and morally. His general character in Kentucky and in Washington was that of an honorable, peaceful, and reliable man who had recently become feeble and emaciated.[124]

"Almost at the End" was the caption the *Louisville Times* carried on its front page denoting the incredible trial was about to come to a conclusion, possibly with a verdict at the end of the week. Altering from the usual pattern of political witnesses testifying before the jury, the defense attorney called upon Miss Millmore, a boardinghouse acquaintance of Sam Donaldson. At dinner on the evening of the tragedy, she had a conversation with Donaldson, his wife, and his sister-in-law. Miss Millmore said Donaldson informed her, before the shooting, Kincaid and Taulbee had exchanged words, and an excited Taulbee had told Kincaid to arm himself. On recall, Donaldson denied this statement furiously, as well as others attributed to him. Attorney Fletcher Johnston, formerly of Lexington, Kentucky, testified just the opposite. Johnston declared he had never heard Taulbee threaten Kincaid, but it had been common talk for many months, especially among Kentuckians. Jay F. Dunham repeated similar testimony concerning Taulbee's threat, "I should have killed Kincaid when he wrote that article about me; and if he ever comes in my path again, I will kill him."[125]

An overwrought female witness was called next to the stand; Miss Emily Kincaid, sister of the defendant, was asked to testify on the physical condition of her brother after the shooting. She was understandably excused from testifying. Following her dismissal was the testimony of yet another correspondent of the *Washington Evening Star* who, upon recall, testified on the day of the shooting he was speaking with Woodbridge who revealed the words spoken

124. "Of Good Repute," *Louisville (Ky.) Times*, 30 March 1891, 1.
125. "Better Arm Yourself," *Louisville (Ky.) Times*, 31 March 1891, 1.

Police officers in Washington, D.C., traveled in vans similar to the one pictured. Several of the men who served at the Sixth and Twelfth Precinct Police Stations were used to transport reporter Charles E. Kincaid to trial.
[Courtesy of the Metropolitan Police Department
of the District of Columbia.]

by Taulbee that unfortunate morning: "You had better arm your-self. You had better be."[126]

Robert Richardson who, for eighteen years, had been in charge of the baths at the House, finished the testimony that day. Rich-ardson attested shortly after the publication of the disgraceful arti-cle, Taulbee came into the bathroom, took a pistol from his pocket, and showed it to Richardson, saying, "I intend to kill Kin-caid, a newspaper (expletive) from Kentucky."[127] Before the prose-cution's ending statement, witnesses, who had already testified, were recalled in court. However, in the middle of this session there was quite a delay in the resumption of the trial as the prosecuting attorney was slow in returning some of the government witnesses

126. Ibid.
127. "The Kincaid Trial," *Kentucky Advocate* (Danville, Ky.), 3 April 1891, 1.

for reexamination. Dr. Lamb, Dr. Bayne, and Dr. Adams again offered medical testimony as to the condition of the body. Dr. Adams presented the only tidbit of new testimony when he stated that he had given Taulbee a drink of whiskey after the shooting. Next, Mr. Lovel and Mr. Coolly, doorkeepers at the Capitol, gave contradictory evidence of their prior testimony. The additional medical witness taking the stand that day was Dr. H. L. Johnson, who testified Taulbee's face was smeared with powder burns or stains on both sides of the nose and spread over a space on the face about four inches in diameter. Johnson also displayed, with the use of a skull, the trajectory of the bullet and condition of the abscess formed as a result of the wound. Dr. James Kerr was also examined and gave important testimony regarding a person's mental condition when suffering from wounds to the brain.

Adding to the general confusion, but offering a needed relief from the depressing testimonies, was the reading of a juror's letter containing an element of romance. The juror, James H. Byram, Jr., a local printer, informed the court he had postponed his wedding for two weeks for this trial. The judge allowed this letter from the prospective bride to be read and those in the courtroom experienced considerable enjoyment at this lighter moment in what had been a protracted, depressing trial.[128] The bride's letter was most attentively heard by Judge Bradley and the jury members; however, the judge did not tolerate any more joviality. He decided not to allow the general public into the courtroom, which was a disappointment to the great number of people who had been attending daily. This action was taken due to the large crowd in the outer space making for too much confusion by whispering, shuffling of feet, and otherwise acting like spectators.

At length, the defendant, Charles E. Kincaid, was requested to take the stand; looking pale and showing ill health, he proceeded

---

128. "An Element of Romance," *Louisville (Ky.) Times*, 2 April 1891, 1.

to answer the questions asked by Judge Bradley. Kincaid detailed the troubles with Taulbee, and how he had avoided him to prevent a difficulty and the eventual shooting. He pointed out in court Taulbee had called him a coward and monkey, and he shot him because he believed it was Taulbee's life or his.[129] Judge Bradley let Kincaid explain his case thoroughly and overruled many objections of the prosecution. Kincaid explained his actions to include his purpose for being on the steps; one purpose was to see Kentucky congressman Isaac H. Goodnight in the restaurant, and the other was to get a cup of coffee, as he was weak. He came upon Taulbee and Donaldson whispering together on the stairs where, at this point, his testimony concurred with most of the previous witnesses.[130]

A mistrial was avoided when a juror, William P. Middleton, a coal delivery man, became seriously ill with an attack of the grippe, and the trial had to be lengthened one day. The juror was helped to maintain his composure with medicines and stimulants so that he could finish the trial. If Middleton had grown worse, incapacitated, or died, it would have resulted in the trial being repeated.[131] In fact, another witness became ill during the trial and had to be put to bed, and it was later discovered the judge was also not well. With Assistant District Attorney Clagett only half way through his argument and the jurors being so ill, the trial was becoming an unfortunate affair with the cold and chilling rain striking down jurors.[132]

After a weekend's rest, the jurors and judge resumed court with the crowd presence becoming larger, as the sunshiny day brought out many local citizens. C. Maurice Smith, counsel for the defendant, continued his arguments and was particularly severe

---

129. Ibid.; "The Kincaid Trial."

130. "Hearing Evidence," *Louisville (Ky.) Times,* 25 March 1891, 1.

131. "LaGrippe Seized a Juryman," *Louisville (Ky.) Times,* 3 April 1891, 1.

132. "Judge and Jurors Ill," *Louisville (Ky.) Times,* 4 April 1891, 1.

The most recognized building in Washington, D.C., is the White House. During the last decade of the nineteenth century, President Benjamin Harrison and his family resided here and oversaw functions of national importance.
[COURTESY OF THE LIBRARY OF CONGRESS ARCHIVES.]

with Donaldson, commenting emphatically upon the fact that he (Donaldson) ran away after the shooting while his friend was bleeding on the steps. His only excuse being he had to return a borrowed book. Smith referred to Donaldson as the "evil genius" of the case.[133] The trial soon became loud again and Judge Bradley refused admittance to the public, with only the lawyers, newspaper representatives, and a few ladies, who had been attending regularly—much to the anger of many spectators who could see empty seats through the windows.

---

133. "Able to Sit," *Louisville (Ky.) Times*, 7 April 1891, 1.

CHAPTER 9

Kincaid Found Not Guilty

DISTRICT ATTORNEY COLE commenced his final argument with the demand that justice be claimed and the law should be vindicated. Cole insisted Kincaid be found guilty of either murder or manslaughter. He had argued Kincaid had malice in his mind when the shot was fired, since he had time to "cool off" before returning for the killing. Cole stressed manslaughter in the hopes the jury would find that acceptable and intimated that the prosecution would find it possible to accept. The prosecuting attorney would not accept self-defense as a plea, as the deceased had not attempted any assault upon the defendant—conceding Taulbee had not done all he could to minimize the tension between them. Clearly, the attorney pointed out

> If Taulbee had meant to kill Kincaid, he would have done it long before that day as he had plenty of opportunities. When he pulled Kincaid's ear, he did so with no intent of bodily harm nor did he when they met on the stairs. Instead, Kincaid was humiliated and went to his room to arm himself with a revolver and sought Taulbee in the Capitol. Kincaid wanted to show the

world that he was not a coward, but that he would return the public opinion of him to a high stature and avenge himself.[134]

Cole also accused Kincaid of laying a set of circumstances for his advantage before the shooting so he would be able to use self-defense as a plea. The brief amount of time transpiring between Kincaid's calling out Taulbee's name and the shot should have proven to the jury that Kincaid had not been assaulted during the time of the shooting.[135]

However, on April 8, 1891, the jury returned a verdict of "not guilty," after deliberating only a few hours, during which time they condensed weeks of testimony into a brief statement read before the judge and courtroom of stalwart observers. After the jury foreman read the verdict before the packed courtroom, Kincaid was able to recompose himself and took the hands of all jurors, giving each one thanks for their belief in

WILSON TALKS.

He Refers To His Opponents Only In Honeyed Phrases,

But Announces Himself For Curtis F. Burnam For Governor.

Bradley Referred To As a "Very Popular Man."

REJOICED AT KINCAID'S ACQUITTAL.

After the verdict was read, announcing Kincaid to be a free man, Honorable John H. Wilson publicly announced he was impressed with Kincaid's demeanor and testimony throughout the trial and rejoiced greatly with the not guilty verdict.

[COURTESY OF THE *LOUISVILLE TIMES* ARCHIVES.]

him. When seen by a *Louisville Times* reporter, John H. Wilson said, "Charley Kincaid made the most favorable appearance on the witness stand of any man I ever saw. His testimony, on his own behalf, was clear and convincing. The jury was favorably impressed, and this

---

134. "Argument Done," *Louisville (Ky.) Times*, 8 April 1891, 1.
135. Ibid.

alone was sufficient to decide the case in his favor."[136]

The next day, newspapers in Kentucky reported the result of the trial with various headlines—all depicting the final outcome of the prolonged trial. The *Kentucky State Journal* editors asserted, "Kincaid Declared a Free Man," with the jury's deliberations lasting only two hours and a half.[137] "Kincaid Not Guilty" was the bold headline reported on that day in Lexington, the jury having reported their unanimous verdict at 8:00 p.m. the previous night.[138] Kincaid's employer, the *Louisville Times*, devoted an entire column for the news of Kincaid's acquittal, even using the word "rejoicing" to describe the verdict of acquittal. The majority of the article concerned Wilson and his accounting of the trial on a return visit to Louisville at the Rafer Hotel. Wilson was used as a witness on behalf of both the prosecution and the defense teams although he was a supporter of Kincaid's and was elated with the verdict.

While some witnesses thought the jury could have reached a decision in a half hour, the long wait must have taken its toll on Kincaid, as he had a brief fainting spell. What transpired in the ballot room was a vote of nine for acquittal, one for manslaughter, and two voted blanks. Reportedly, there was only a few minutes delay before all the jurors voted for acquittal. Some of the jurors, who spoke of the case after they were discharged, said by the time the testimony for the defense was complete, more than a majority of the jurors had practically reached the conclusion Kincaid was not guilty. In their opinion, Kincaid fired the shot in self-defense.[139]

Charles Eustis Kincaid had previously served the government as a U.S. consular agent in Lancashire, England.[140] Kincaid returned to Kentucky to serve on the Kentucky Railroad Commission and

---

136. "Wilson Talks," *Louisville (Ky.) Times*, 9 April 1891, 1.

137. "Kincaid Declared a Free Man," *Kentucky State Journal* (Frankfort, Ky.), 9 April 1891, 1.

138. "Kincaid Not Guilty," *Kentucky Leader* (Lexington, Ky.), 9 April 1891, 1.

139. "After Acquittal," *Louisville (Ky.) Times*, 9 April 1891, 1.

140. "Shooting Grew Out of Scandal Published by Kincaid," *Washington (D.C.) Herald*, 3 November 1906.

resumed his duties as a correspondent for several noted newspapers in New York, San Francisco, and Louisville. Death ended his career in November 1906 at age fifty-one while he was a reporter with the *Cincinnati Enquirer*. Noted in his obituary published in the *Washington Herald* was a brief description of the mayhem following the shooting in the Capitol some sixteen years before, "A crowd surged around the wounded man. Blood rushed from Taulbee's nose and mouth. Taulbee was partially on the floor as Kincaid stood over him. Kincaid was nervous and excited, grew faint and was practically carried to the House Public Buildings and Grounds committee room while Taulbee was taken to Providence Hospital in a carriage. From the Capitol, Kincaid was led first to the Sixth Street Police Station on New Jersey Avenue. The trial was exciting and Kincaid was eventually acquitted on a self-defense plea, as the jury decided Taulbee had baited Kincaid at every opportunity, threatening him with bodily harm. Taulbee was a big, muscular man, powerfully built, a true Kentucky mountaineer. Kincaid was slight and suffered from a disease."[141]

The more noncommittal newspapers in eastern Kentucky interpreted the verdict in a more affronted manner. "An Outrage of Justice" was the headline used by the *Hazel Green Herald*, which proffered the acquittal of Charles E. Kincaid for the murder of Hon. William Preston Taulbee served as an indignation to the citizens of that district. The newspaper's editor believed the prosecution had not laid out the trial testimony so the jury could have understood it better and for admitting hearsay evidence so often admitted in court. This view was clearly expressed for the readers: "In short, public opinion looks upon the prosecution as a judicial farce. Kincaid is free under the laws of man . . . but if his conscious be guilt-stained, his heart will harbor a horrible hell . . . the matter rests with God."[142] Understandably, the residents of eastern Kentucky and family members of William Preston Taulbee were embarrassed with the scandalous accusations, as well as angered with what they considered an extreme

---

141. "Recalls a Tragedy," *Washington (D.C.) Herald*, 3 November 1906, 2.
142. "Kincaid is a Free Man," *Hazel Green (Ky.) Herald*, 17 April 1891, 2.

Sabina Ann Taulbee DeBusk, a niece of Representative William P. Taulbee, continued to keep the large Taulbee family and its descendants concentrating on the positive contributions they had made to Kentucky.
[COURTESY OF THE DEBUSK-TAULBEE FAMILY COLLECTION.]

miscarriage of justice.

Certainly when the news media in the late 1880s concentrated its columns on "gossip," there caused a plethora of scandalous information to be dispersed to a waiting audience, particularly in Washington, D.C. With both men attempting to "save face," there seemed no recourse but an open airing of their differences and a continuation of public embarrassment at each other's expense. Obviously, from the first moments after hearing the gun report, the potential witnesses were reacting with such differing emotions and recollections it might

*Former Representative William P. Taulbee's funeral was observed in this Methodist
Church located in Hazel Green. Those in attendance certainly concentrated their
thoughts on Taulbee's widow, their five surviving sons, and the political contributions he
had made during his terms in office.*
[COURTESY OF ELIZABETH TAHERI.]

have become impossible a year later for a jury to distinguish fact from
sensationalism. The highly charged atmosphere of the Capitol that
day did not lesson with the conclusion of the trial. Nevertheless, perhaps this renewed examination of the specifics of this murder case will
allow the "ghost" of the Capitol to leave and the harassment of the
Fourth Estate to cease. Or, is the verdict still out—capital murder or
Capitol mayhem?

*Representative William P. Taulbee is buried near Adele in Morgan County, Kentucky, at
a family cemetery where his grave is marked with this tombstone.*
[COURTESY OF ELIZABETH TAHERI.]

Bibliography

Helton, Roy. "Old Christmas." In *Lonesome Water*. New York: Harper and Brothers, 1930.

————, "Old Christmas." In *Adventures in Appreciation*. San Diego: Harcourt, Brace, 1958.

Kleber, John E., editor. *The Kentucky Encyclopedia*. Lexington, Ky.: University Press of Kentucky, 1992.

Klotter, James C. *Kentucky Justice, Southern Honor, and American Manhood: Understanding the Life and Death of Richard Reid*. Baton Rouge, La.: Louisiana State University Press, 2003.

Krepp, Tim. "The Bloody Steps." In *Capitol Hill Haunts*. Charleston, S.C.: The History Press, 2012.

McAfee, John J. "Hon. William Preston Taulbee." In *Kentucky Politicians: Sketches of Representative Corn-crackers and Other Miscellany*. Louisville, Ky.: Courier-Journal Job Printing Co., 1886.

National Cyclopaedia. New York: James T. White and Co., 1910.

Pohl, Robert S. *Wicked Capitol Hill: An Unruly History of Behaving Badly*. Charleston, W.Va.: History Press, 2012.

Sylvester, Richard. "Kincaid-Taulbee Tragedy." In *District of Columbia Police: A Retrospect of the Police Organizations*. Washington, D.C.: Gibson Brothers, 1894.

"Taulbee Family." In *Early and Modern History of Wolfe County*. Borderland

Books, 1972.

Taulbee, Rose. *The Family: Taulbee* . . . . Bloomington, Ill.: private printing, 2000.

Index

About the Author

CAROLINE R. MILLER lives in Augusta, Kentucky, and is a retired English teacher. Currently she is a researcher and writer for the Bracken County Historical Society. Among her many articles and books are *Grapevine Dispatch: The Voice of Antislavery Messages*, Images of America Series: *Bracken County, An American Nurse Ascending the Alps in Albania, Dachau Album*, eight volumes of compilations of slave records, five volumes of World War II letters, and a recent yearbook titled *Veterans of Bracken County, Kentucky*.